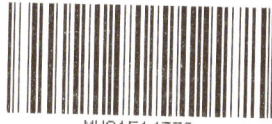

THE
BIBLE
IN A
YEAR

Study Guide

Fr. Mike Schmitz

Claire Couche

ASCENSION

West Chester, Pennsylvania

Excerpts from the English translation of the *Catechism of the Catholic Church* for use in the United States of America © 1994 United States Catholic Conference, Inc.–Libreria Editrice Vaticana. Used by permission. English translation of the *Catechism of the Catholic Church: Modifications from the Editio Typica* © 1997 United States Conference of Catholic Bishops–Libreria Editrice Vaticana. All italics are original emphasis.

Scripture passages are from the Revised Standard Version of the Bible–Second Catholic Edition (Ignatius Edition) © 2006 National Council of the Churches of Christ in the United States of America. Used by permission. All rights reserved.

Ascension
PO Box 1990
West Chester, PA 19380
1-800-376-0520
ascensionpress.com

Design by Ashley Dias

25 26 27 28 29 5 4 3 2 1

Printed in the United States of America

ISBN 979-8-89276-102-4 (trade book)
ISBN 979-8-89276-103-1 (e-book)

CONTENTS

The Bible Timeline divides the pages of the Bible into 12 time periods and shows how the different books fit into the time periods to tell the story.

Each *Great Adventure Bible Timeline* period has been assigned a color to represent what happened during this stage of the story of salvation:

Period	Color
Early World	Turquoise, the color of the earth viewed from space
Patriarchs	Burgundy, representing God's blood covenant with Abraham
Egypt and Exodus	Red, the color of the Red Sea
Desert Wanderings	Tan, the color of the desert
Conquest and Judges	Green, the color of the hills of Canaan
Royal Kingdom	Purple, the color of royalty
Divided Kingdom	Black, representing Israel's darkest period
Exile	Baby blue, symbolizing Judah "singing the blues" in Babylon
Return	Yellow, symbolizing Judah's return home to brighter days
Maccabean Revolt	Orange, the color of the fire in the lamps in the purified Temple
Messianic Fulfillment	Gold, representing the gifts of the Magi
The Church	White, the color of the spotless Bride of Christ

*Note: Each week is color-coded with the *Great Adventure Bible Timeline* period it *starts* in.

HOW TO USE THIS
BIBLE IN A YEAR STUDY GUIDE

This study guide offers various ways to help you dive deeper into God's Word and apply Scripture to your life in an actionable way. This book will guide you through *The Bible in a Year*® podcast week by week, offering a variety of features, including **prayers**, **reflection with Scripture**, **weekly challenges**, a **saint of the week**, and *Catechism* **connections**.

- **Opening and Closing Prayers:** Each week begins and ends with a prayer. These prayers may sound familiar, as they reflect the prayers offered by Fr. Mike Schmitz in *The Bible in a Year* podcast. Whether you are using this book on your own or as part of a group, these prayers serve as holy bookends for your time of reflection on Scripture.

- **Reflection with Scripture:** You will find a variety of reflection prompts for each week of podcast content. These reflection questions have been thoughtfully created and curated for you so that you don't need to come up with them on your own, whether you are leading a group or looking for deeper personal reflection. Some of these prompts are ideal for discussion in a group setting, others are questions to reflect on individually, and some prompts may spark curiosity and further research. The reflection questions take into account the Scripture content being discussed in the podcast episodes each week and highlight some of the key points to consider.

- **Weekly Challenge:** There are always little things we can do to bring God's Word into our lives more concretely. This section is intended to inspire ideas for taking a key point or insight from the weekly podcast content and transforming listening into action in a meaningful way.

- **Group Activity:** If you are using this guide in a group setting, this section invites you to share more deeply with your group members and experience your faith in the context of a community that revolves around Scripture.
- **Saint of the Week:** Each week includes the name and feast day of a saint. This section offers a holy example of someone who has lived a life of faith and reminds us to pray for the intercession of the saints who have walked this journey before us.
- **Note of Hope:** While often challenging, God's Word is ultimately a message of hope. This section is intended to help you reflect on what God promises when you place him at the center of your life. It is a reminder of what it truly means to live a life through the lens of faith.
- **Prayer Intentions:** Drawing from the podcast content from the week, this section offers suggestions to help you remember others in your prayers. Whether you are using this guide on your own or as part of a group, this section is a great way to offer your prayers for those in need.
- **Catechism Connection:** The Bible and the *Catechism of the Catholic Church* are closely tied together within our Catholic Faith. In this section, paragraphs from the *Catechism* are highlighted to help connect the messages of Scripture to the tenets of our Faith.
- **Scripture Verse to Remember:** One Bible verse has been selected for each week as a key reminder and a message that you can carry with you throughout the week.

By using this *Bible in a Year Study Guide*, you are embarking on a transformative journey through Scripture, deepening your faith, and growing in your relationship with God. This guide equips you not only to understand Scripture but also to apply its message in your daily life. As you move through the weeks, we hope that you discover wisdom, encouragement, and a renewed sense of purpose in God's Word. May this journey strengthen your faith and inspire you to share the love of Christ with all those you encounter.

A MESSAGE FROM FR. MIKE

Hi, this is Fr. Mike Schmitz, and I just want to say how excited I am that you're holding this *Bible in a Year Study Guide* in your hands.

This book isn't just a companion—it's an invitation. An invitation not only to **read the Bible** but to **wrestle with it, pray with it**, and **let it shape your heart**. Because the Bible isn't just an ancient book of wisdom—it's the **living Word of God**, and through it, God is still speaking directly to **you**.

This study guide is designed to help you go deeper. It will walk with you, week by week, into a more intimate relationship with the Lord. It encourages you to engage with Scripture not just intellectually but **personally**—to ask honest questions, to sit with difficult passages, and to let the Holy Spirit guide you into greater clarity and conviction.

And if you're using this in a group, even better! There is so much value in coming together as a community to share what God is doing in each of our hearts through his Word. These conversations can spark real transformation and remind us that **we are not alone** on this journey.

So whether you're on day 1 or day 101, and whether you're doing this on your own or in a small group, I just want to encourage you to **keep going**. God is doing something powerful in your life. You may not always feel it, but he is. His Word never returns empty—and he is not done with you yet.

Let's dive in, and let's keep saying yes to the adventure of walking with God through his Word.

Opening Prayer

Father in heaven, we give you glory, and we love you. Thank you for sharing your Word with us; for giving us a clear vision of how you created this world and how we allowed sin to enter into it. Thank you for not abandoning us in our woundedness but always following us into the darkness so that you can be our light. Father, we give you thanks and praise. In Jesus' name, we pray. Amen.

Reflection with Scripture

☐ 1. Have you ever read the entire Bible? Do you read Scripture daily, or is this a new experience for you? What are some reasons you want to commit to listening to *The Bible in a Year*—what is your "why"?

☐ 2. Pope Benedict XVI writes that "God's way of loving becomes the measure of human love."[1] Whether or not we are called to marriage, we were created in love, to love. Do we measure how we love others—our spouse, friends, neighbors, fellow parishioners, strangers, and those in need—by the way God loves us?

☐ 3. Fr. Mike explains that before the Fall, God's plan was for man to labor like him, to have leisure like him, and to love like him. In reflecting on your current routine, how are you fulfilling each of these three objectives? Are you lacking in one of these areas? What can you do to better live out each of these?

---

1. Benedict XVI, *Deus Caritas Est* (December 25, 2005), 11, vatican.va.

☐ 4. After the Fall, Adam and Eve "hid themselves from the presence of the LORD God" (Genesis 3:8). What are some ways God seeks us in our day-to-day lives? Why might we be afraid to fully reveal ourselves to him? How can we better walk with him, with all our heart, mind, and soul exposed to his love?

☐ 5. Psalm 136:1 reminds us that "his mercy endures for ever," and Christ calls the merciful blessed. What are some ways we can extend mercy to others? The book of Job begins with extreme pain and loss, yet "in all this Job did not sin or charge God with wrong" (Job 1:22). What is my first reaction to pain and loss?

Weekly Challenge

If you don't know your Baptism date, contact the parish where you were baptized and ask for that information. Or ask a family member who may know the date. Write the date on the calendar, and when that day comes, celebrate it! Some ideas are attending Mass that day, asking for a special blessing from your parish priest, praying a Rosary, or having a special meal.

Group Activity

The floodwaters in Noah's story prefigure the waters of our Baptism and our new creation in Christ. Ask group members if they know the date they were baptized and look up what saint's feast day that lands on. Brainstorm ways to celebrate the day. On index cards, have each person in the group write one word or phrase that they associate with Baptism (for example, "new life," "forgiveness," "grace"). Afterward, invite each group member to share their word and why they chose it.

Note of Hope

We are created in God's image and likeness. In him we move and live and have our being. He created us in love, for love, to love. He is our Divine Bridegroom and friend—he is our Savior. He knows every beat of our heart, every hair on our head, every heartache, every joy, every worry, every pain, every dream, every goal. We have no need to run and hide from the One who knows us so intimately, our Creator. This week, let us ask God to reveal where we resist "walking with him." Let us remember that he is Mercy and Love. He is trustworthy, gentle, and kind.

SCRIPTURE VERSE TO REMEMBER

*"I will sing to the LORD as long as I live;
I will sing praise to my God while I have being."*
PSALM 104:33

Prayer Intentions

Response (R): God the Father, King of Creation, King of my Heart, have mercy on us!

For all marriages, that spouses may measure their love by God's way of loving: *R.*

That our passions, hobbies, and activities may all reflect God's creativity and light: *R.*

That we may always trust in God's goodness and promises: *R.*

That we may always make God's name known: *R.*

That in extending mercy we may receive his mercy: *R.*

When our pain and loss lead to bitterness and discouragement: *R.*

When we are tempted to hide ourselves from his ever-seeking love: *R.*

Let us pray: Lord, thank you for the graces and blessings prepared for us this year in your Word. May we walk in the garden with you and allow you to tend and till our hearts.

St. André Bessette, through the intercession of your heavenly friend, St. Joseph, pray for us and all in need, especially those who are sick, marginalized, and in need of healing. **Feast Day: January 6**

Catechism Connection

These paragraphs in the *Catechism* may be helpful for reflection on the Scripture read this week in *The Bible in a Year*: CCC 54–55, 293, 357, 362, 1426, 2176

Highlights from the *Catechism*:
- "God ... provides men with constant evidence of himself in created realities" (CCC 54).
- "The human person, created in the image of God, is a being at once corporeal and spiritual ... Man, whole and entire, is ... *willed* by God" (CCC 362).

Closing Prayer

Father in heaven, thank you so much for bringing us here. Thank you for speaking your Word to us. Thank you for revealing your heart to us as you do whenever we hear or read your Word. Lord, you enlighten our minds and enlighten our eyes. You give fire to our hearts and show us how to love. Help us to trust you this day and every day. In Jesus' name, we pray. Amen.

Opening Prayer

Lord God, in the midst of confusion and suffering, we ask that you give us your Truth. Sometimes we don't want answers as much as we want you, so please give us yourself and your peace. I ask that you please give those suffering the confidence, trust, and faith in you. Help them know that, above all things, you are faithful, and your love is unstoppable. You are good. We praise you, in Jesus' name. Amen.

Reflection with Scripture

☐ 1. We hear Job's friend, Eliphaz, try to make sense out of Job's suffering. So often in suffering, someone's presence and silence are needed the most. Is there someone in our life who is suffering? How can we be present to that person?

☐ 2. What is our reaction to God's destruction in the Old Testament? God is infinitely just and merciful. Are we fearful of God the Father, seeing him as vengeful? Or do we see him as a good, merciful Father, our Creator?

☐ 3. Even though Abraham intimately knows the goodness of God, he succumbs to fear and lies to Abimelech about his true relationship with Sarah. What is my biggest fear right now? In what ways am I allowing that fear to reign in my life and even control my relationships with those around me?

☐ 4. Sarah experienced deep jealousy in what should have been a time of joy. Do I tend to respond properly to the people, goods, and values before me? Or do I often react and let my emotions take control over my will? Is there someone I have treated poorly because of my jealousy?

☐ 5. When we sin, it is as if we are trading in our inheritance like Esau. We often choose lesser goods, or even evils, over God's goodness. We are tempted to create idols of food, social media, status, and luxury instead of worshiping God and properly ordering our lives. Is there something or someone in my life I have idolized and traded my true inheritance for? Name it and ask God to break those chains and reign King of your heart.

Weekly Challenge

Though there are specific times we are called to offer our advice, counsel, and commentary, there are moments when our silence and presence are needed. There are times throughout each day that we may be tempted to speak when silence would be the higher good.

Every morning this week, ask the Holy Spirit to guide your speech. As an act of trust and humility, hold back a comment that would be unnecessary or even harmful (such as a quip, criticism, or words of self-promotion).

Group Activity

Read paragraphs 2735–2737 on prayer in the *Catechism of the Catholic Church*. The topic is, "Why do we complain of not being heard?" Like Job, we often demand immediate results and answers from our petitions to God. After reading these paragraphs, discuss different methods of prayer that have brought you peace and have deepened your trust in God's timing, goodness, and love for you.

Note of Hope

Abraham, the Father of Faith, shows us that faith leads to trust in God's plan and will for our lives. At each moment of every day, we have the opportunity to place our trust in God. That trust leads to greater love of God and, in turn, our neighbor. In his book *Five Loaves and Two Fish*, Venerable Francis-Xavier Nguyễn Văn Thuận instructs us:

> How does one reach this intensity of love in the present moment? I simply recall that I must live each day, each moment as if it were the last one of my life. I leave aside everything accidental and concentrate only on the essential; then each word, each gesture, each telephone call, and each decision I make is the most beautiful of my life. I give my love to everyone, my smile to everyone; I am afraid of wasting even one second by living it without meaning.[2]

A beautiful fruit of our faith in God in every moment is our love for our neighbor in the present moment.

SCRIPTURE VERSE TO REMEMBER

"Abraham said, 'God will provide himself the lamb for a burnt offering, my son.' So they went both of them together."
GENESIS 22:8

Prayer Intentions

Response (R): Lord, in your merciful love, heal our wounds.
When I am tempted to deceive those around me out of fear: **R.**
When my yearning turns into jealousy: **R.**

---

2. See Francis-Xavier Nguyễn Văn Thuận, *Five Loaves and Two Fish* (Boston: Pauline Books, 2003).

For healing of any wounds we received from family members: **R.**

In reparation for any wounds we have inflicted on family members: **R.**

When we choose lesser goods instead of your goodness: **R.**

For the times I have created an idol out of food, social media, status, or luxury: **R.**

For the graces and blessings prepared for us this year in your Word: **R.**

Catechism Connection

These paragraphs in the *Catechism* may be helpful for reflection on the Scripture read this week in *The Bible in a Year*: CCC 144, 146, 1814, 2570, 2847

Highlight from the *Catechism*:

- "Faith is the theological virtue by which we believe in God and believe all that he has said and revealed to us, and that Holy Church proposes for our belief, because he is truth itself" (CCC 1814).

Closing Prayer

God in heaven, we give you praise and glory. We thank you for giving us your Word. It is your heart that you revealed to us in your Word, that our hearts become like yours. Help us to love what you love, to despise what you despise, and to live as you have willed us to live and as you have made it possible for us to live by your grace. May you be glorified in all things this day. In Jesus' name, we pray. Amen.

Reflection with Scripture

☐ 1. Is there someone I am getting tired of sitting with in his or her grief? In what way can I show them love this week?

☐ 2. Silence can make us uncomfortable, but God speaks through silence. In his apostolic exhortation *Verbum Domini*, Pope Benedict XVI details this holy silence: "Only in silence can the word of God find a home in us."[3] In what areas of our life do we add noise where there should be silence?

☐ 3. Rachel is loved by her husband, while Leah is merely tolerated by her husband. Fr. Mike reminds us that many of us experience this in some way, too. We feel that others should rightfully love us, yet we sense that they are just tolerating us. How can we be on guard against merely tolerating those around us and

---

3. Benedict XVI, *Verbum Domini* (September 30, 2010), 66, vatican.va.

instead show them true charity? In what ways can we embrace the truth that God truly loves us; he doesn't just "tolerate" us?

☐ 4. God allows us to choose brokenness and even works with us in our brokenness. God uses everything when we surrender it to him. Is there something that I am ashamed to hand over to him? That I feel is too broken for him to work with? He is faithful and steadfast. No sin is too big for him and his Merciful Love.

☐ 5. When others suffer, our immediate reaction is often to come up with an answer for their suffering. Are we too quick to talk instead of listen? What are some ways we can be more present to those in need and genuinely hear them? When is it better to offer advice, and when is it better not to?

Weekly Challenge
Reach out to someone you know who is grieving, suffering, or struggling this week. It could be a simple text, email, or phone call. Or, send a note or flowers.

Group Activity
Have each person write down one area of their life where they are struggling and suffering. Share with the group if comfortable. End the discussion by praying for each person by name and their struggle and suffering.

Note of Hope

Lord, all that you permit, all that you allow is for your greater glory, our salvation, and the salvation of the world. May we always choose you—in our joy, in our sorrow, in our temptation, and in our charity. When we do not, and we turn toward idols, please give us the grace to know that you give us chance after chance and that you are always there, waiting for us to return to you. Help us to return to you always.

SCRIPTURE VERSE TO REMEMBER

*"For I know that my Redeemer lives,
and at last he will stand upon the earth."*
JOB 19:25

Prayer Intentions

Response (R): The gain of wisdom and understanding is better than gold.

When we are tempted to turn to idols instead of you, help us to remember: *R.*

When we choose brokenness, let us return to you and recall: *R.*

When we betray the ones we love for the "coins" of sin, help us repent and remember: *R.*

When we are betrayed, lonely, and hurt, let us be mindful: *R.*

For the graces and blessings prepared for us this year in your Word: *R.*

St. Agnes, pray for us and all in need, especially engaged couples and victims of sexual abuse.
Feast Day: January 21

Catechism Connection

These paragraphs in the *Catechism* may be helpful for reflection on the Scripture read this week in *The Bible in a Year*: CCC 1500–1501, 2448, 2658, 2732

Highlight from the *Catechism*:

- "The most common yet most hidden temptation is our *lack of faith*. It expresses itself less by declared incredulity than by our actual preferences" (CCC 2732).

Closing Prayer

God in heaven, we thank you. We thank you for your Word. We thank you for revealing your heart to us. We thank you for heroes, for people who are faithful, like Job and Joseph. Help us to be the kind of men and women who know your name and your commands and have the ability and grace, the perseverance and persistence, and the confidence and trust in you to do your will in all things. We make this prayer in Jesus' name. Amen.

Reflection with Scripture

☐ 1. Joseph is overwhelmed at the sight of his brothers after years apart and their betrayal of him. He "sought a place to weep" (Genesis 43:30). He deeply desires reconciliation. What is something that strikes you about Joseph's honest reaction?

☐ 2. When Joseph forgives his brothers, he tells them that God brought good from their sinful actions (see Genesis 50:20). Reflecting on your life and your own story, when and how has God brought beauty and forgiveness out of a painful situation through his permissive will? How can we enter into this mystery of trust?

☐ 3. Exodus opens with a new Pharaoh who enslaves the Israelites and subjects them to a life of oppression. What had been a hospitable land for four hundred years is now a land of enslavement. Is there something in your life that was once a source of true joy but is now misused and has become an idol? What things in your life are you enslaved to? People's opinions, your phone, social media, your schedule, your looks, the fear of aging, the search for wealth and power?

☐ 4. Moses' reaction is one of fear and doubt when God instructs him on his mission to save his people. God responds to this fear by saying, "But I will be with you" (Exodus 3:12). When we feel inadequate to carry out God's plan for our lives, do we allow fear and doubt to overcome us, or do we trust in God's promise that he is with us?

☐ 5. In Psalm 16, we hear about God's "delight" in those who are holy. Do we firmly believe God delights in us? What are some parts of our own personality, character, and life, and the character traits of those around us, that God delights in? How can we remind others of God's delight in them?

Weekly Challenge

Learn about a devotion to St. Joseph this week. Here are some ideas:

- Seven Sorrows and Seven Joys Devotion
- Seven Sundays Devotion
- Cord of St. Joseph
- Novena of the Holy Cloak of St. Joseph
- Consecration to Jesus through St. Joseph
- Litany of St. Joseph

Group Activity

This week starts out with a call to "Go to Joseph": *Ite ad Joseph* (see Genesis 41:55). Though spoken about Joseph of the Old Testament, these words point to St. Joseph of the New Testament, who led, protected, and sacrificed for Mother Mary and Jesus. Discuss your relationship with your spiritual father, St. Joseph. Do you have one? What is one way to grow closer to him?

Note of Hope

This week, Joseph of the Old Testament teaches us that even in the midst of betrayal and deep pain, God brings about beauty and healing. When we trust in God's timing and his providential love, we are imitating both Josephs, from the Old and the New Testaments. Though it may often seem a mystery, the suffering we all experience in life is often an opportunity for God to bring about his greater glory in the world, in the lives of those around us, and in our own lives.

SCRIPTURE VERSE TO REMEMBER

"I know that you can do all things,
and that no purpose of yours can be thwarted."
JOB 42:2

Prayer Intentions

Response (R): St. Joseph, pray for us.
When we are afraid: *R.*
When we are discouraged: *R.*
When we lack confidence: *R.*
When we are faced with suffering: *R.*
When we feel inadequate to carry out God's plan for our lives: *R.*
In our joys: *R.*
In our triumphs: *R.*
In our relationships: *R.*
During this year spent in God's Word: *R.*

Catechism Connection

These paragraphs in the *Catechism* may be helpful for reflection on the Scripture read this week in *The Bible in a Year*: CCC 312–313, 800

Highlight from the *Catechism*:

- "God in his almighty providence can bring a good from the consequences of an evil, even a moral evil, caused by his creatures … St. Catherine of Siena said to 'those who are scandalized and rebel against what happens to them': 'Everything comes from love, all is ordained for the salvation of man, God does nothing without this goal in mind'" (CCC 312–313).

Closing Prayer

Father in heaven, we thank you once again. We thank you for your Word. We thank you for the gift of yourself. We thank you for being with us with your grace. We know that we can trust you. In all things, we know that we can rely upon you at every moment of our lives. And so, at this moment, and with these things in our lives, we trust you. We declare that you are good. We declare that you are faithful. We receive your love, and we rest in your peace. In Jesus' name, we pray. Amen.

Opening Prayer

Father in heaven, we give you praise; we thank you so much. Thank you for your Word, and thank you for how you reveal that you fight for your people. You fight for us. Also, Lord, you reveal that you want us. You desire us. You are the God who is just, but you are even more than just; you are merciful. More than mercy, you are love. And so, Lord God, we ask that you please visit us with your mercy, with your justice, and with your love. Help us to receive your justice. Help us to receive your love and mercy. In Jesus' name, we pray. Amen.

Reflection with Scripture

☐ 1. When God sends Moses on his mission, Moses objects by saying that he finds speaking difficult (see Exodus 4:10). We are often hesitant to share the Good News. How can we improve our confidence in speaking the Gospel? Is it greater trust in God? Is it learning about the Faith more? Is it overcoming pride?

☐ 2. Fr. Mike talks about how the Israelites are frustrated with Moses and Aaron, saying that they have "interrupted their lives." They were afraid to break away from the slavery of work in order to worship. Do I share this same fear? What are ways I can set aside time each Sunday to properly worship?

☐ 3. God sends ten plagues when Pharaoh refuses to let the Israelites go. These plagues correspond to the false gods of Egypt. This is important for the Israelites to witness because they have dwelt for four hundred years in Egypt and were influenced by the Egyptians' polytheism. Who do I allow myself to "dwell" with? Who are my closest friends? Do they have a good influence on me? Do I influence my friends to do good?

☐ 4. The Israelites were given specific instructions about how to prepare and eat the Passover meal. When we participate in the Mass, how can we honor and acknowledge the meaning behind each ritual and practice?

☐ 5. When the Red Sea parts and Moses and the Israelites cross it, we see God making a way for his people in a desperate situation that appears hopeless. When is a time God has made a way for us or our loved ones in a seemingly hopeless situation?

....

Weekly Challenge

Every day this week, pray for a child you know (your own child, a friend's child, a student, or a young person in your parish or community). Pray that he or she may grow in faith, hope, and charity. Set aside a specific time each day to ask God to help this child grow in virtue and holiness.

Group Activity

Ask the members of the group to think about the children who have been entrusted to them. Invite them to share how they pass down the Faith to these children. What methods work well, and what methods are challenging?

Note of Hope

Throughout the trials and suffering that Moses and the Israelites experienced, God was there protecting and leading them. He delivered them from a life of enslavement and brought them into a new life of freedom. When we surrender in trust to God, we allow God to lead us into a life of joy and liberty. God's faithfulness leads to our freedom. He is the Way and will always provide a way for us.

SCRIPTURE VERSE TO REMEMBER

*"The Lord will fight for you,
and you have only to be still."*
EXODUS 14:14

Prayer Intentions

Response (R): Deliver us, Lord.
From resisting the call to do good: *R.*
From the bondage of sin: *R.*
From all anxiety and feelings of hopelessness: *R.*
In situations that appear desperate: *R.*
From our self-reliance: *R.*
From our self-doubt: *R.*
From illness: *R.*
From temptation during this year spent with your Word: *R.*

Catechism Connection

These paragraphs in the *Catechism* may be helpful for reflection on the Scripture read this week in *The Bible in a Year*: CCC 1093–1094, 1334, 2226

Highlights from the *Catechism*:

- "In the sacramental economy the Holy Spirit fulfills what was prefigured in *the Old Covenant* ... Thus the flood and Noah's ark prefigured salvation by Baptism, as did the cloud and the crossing of the Red Sea" (CCC 1093–1094).
- "*Education in the faith* by the parents should begin in the child's earliest years" (CCC 2226).

Closing Prayer

Father in heaven, we thank you for fighting for your people. You revealed to us in Exodus that you not only see us, but you also know us. You know our plea and our plight, and you answer our prayers by fighting for us. You continue to give us your grace and to call us closer to your heart. Help us always to say yes to you. We ask this prayer through the intercession of the Blessed Virgin Mary, all the saints, and in the mighty name of our God and Lord, Jesus Christ. Amen.

Opening Prayer

Father in heaven, we give you praise. We thank you so much for your Word. We thank you for the gift of revealing your heart to us through Scripture, and we ask that you please let your Scripture and your grace conform our minds to your mind, that we may see things as you see them. Conform our hearts to your heart so we can love things as you love them. Help us to turn away from what kills us and help us turn toward you who gives us life. In Jesus' name, we pray. Amen.

Reflection with Scripture

☐ 1. The Israelites murmured against Moses. In this context, to murmur means to express discontent. Who do we "murmur against" unjustly? When do we allow frustration to make us discontented? How can we respond with patience instead of grumbling?

☐ 2. Fr. Mike talks about how God is not just leading and caring for his people; he is also training them. He is teaching them who he is and how much they can trust in him. In what areas of your life is God refining you? Are you receptive to the growth he desires for you in the challenges he allows?

☐ 3. Moses' father-in-law sees that if Moses continues to try to oversee everything without more help, he will wear himself out, "for the thing is too heavy for you; you are not able to perform it alone" (Exodus 18:18) Is there an area in your life that you need help with, or have you experienced this in the past? In what ways would your life change if you asked for assistance?

☐ 4. Which of the Ten Commandments is the most challenging for me? How can I take steps to open my mind and heart to God's love and law in this area?

☐ 5. Fr. Mike reminds us that before giving the commandments, God establishes a covenant. He desires a relationship before the rules. How can we apply this to our own relationships? Is there a person in our life God is calling us to create a relationship with before we set out to be an instrument in their conversion of heart?

....

Weekly Challenge

Pick one of the Ten Commandments and think of an act of charity you can do to deepen your observance of that commandment. Here are some ideas:

- Remember to keep holy the LORD's Day: Offer to give someone a ride to Mass.
- Honor your father and your mother: If your parents are living, write them a card or call them. If they are deceased, bring flowers to their burial site or light a candle at church and pray for their souls.
- You shall not kill: Donate items to a local pro-life organization.

Group Activity

If a priest is available, ask him to lead your group in an examination of conscience based on each of the Ten Commandments. If a priest is not available, invite a group member to lead this examination.

Note of Hope

Written into each of God's commandments for us is a life of freedom. Here lies a mysterious paradox: We are truly free when we obey him. This life of freedom does not mean a life free from suffering; rather, it is a life of deep meaning within both suffering and joy. He came to set us, the captives, free. Let us remember that no sin is too big for his mercy. Let us run to him and be free.

SCRIPTURE VERSE TO REMEMBER

*"The Lord is my strength and my song,
and he has become my salvation; this is my God,
and I will praise him, my father's God, and I will exalt him."*
EXODUS 15:2

Prayer Intentions

Response (R): O Lord, in your merciful love, forgive us.
When we fall into sin: **R.**
When we succumb to the temptation of pride and self-reliance: **R.**
For the times we ignore those in need: **R.**
For the times we choose things over you: **R.**
When we rebel against your goodness: **R.**
During this year spent with your Word: **R.**

Catechism Connection

These paragraphs in the *Catechism* may be helpful for reflection on the Scripture read this week in *The Bible in a Year*: CCC 1454, 2084, 2464, 2520

Highlight from the *Catechism*:

- "Chastity lets us love with upright and undivided heart" (CCC 2520).

Closing Prayer

Father in heaven, we thank you for your Word. We thank you for this great prayer that reminds us of all that you have done in our lives. Lord God, one of the big temptations we all have is to forget what you have done; to forget your might, your goodness, and your love for us; to forget that you have fought for us. In so many ways and at so many times, you remind us that the Lord will fight for us; all we have to do is keep still. Psalm 78 reminds us of the need for us to remember how good we are and to remember how fickle we can be. Lord God, please help us. If we have been false to you, help us to be true to you now. If we have strayed, please find us and bring us back to your heart. If we have run away from you, we give you permission right now to take hold of our hands and bring us back to you. Bring us back home. Bring us back to you who are good, who fight for us, who love us. Lord God, we make this prayer in the mighty name of Jesus Christ our Lord. Amen.

Opening Prayer

Father in heaven, we praise you not only for your future deliverance for us but also for what you've done for us in the past. We thank you for the gift of worship, for revealing your heart to us, and for revealing how we are to approach you. Without this, we would be lost and have no idea how you desire us to live truly in freedom and in holiness. Because you are holy, you call us to be holy and make it possible by your grace. Help us to choose holiness, to choose you, and to glorify you today. In Jesus' name, we pray. Amen.

Reflection with Scripture

☐ 1. Reflecting on Psalm 119:143, do we delight in God's commandments? Or do we see them as a burden? How can we grow in deeper love of God's commandments in our daily life?

☐ 2. Fr. Mike reminds us that we are set apart, consecrated, and sacred. Therefore, the work we do, no matter how ordinary, becomes extraordinary because the One who is doing it has been sanctified. Our work is transformed when we live a life in Christ. Do you see your work as a path to holiness? How can you bring the extraordinary life of Christ within your work?

☐ 3. When the golden calf was made, the Israelites had traded in their uncertainty for control. So often we want to control a situation or a person, and can even make an idol of that desire for control. Or, we create an idol of things we can control. Do I trade in my fear and uncertainty for control? Or do I trust God within the uncertainty?

☐ 4. Even after seeing the miraculous and mighty acts of God, the Israelites were quick to turn away from God. Is our own faith planted deeply in fertile ground? Or are we quick to "drop" our faith depending on who we are surrounded with, what friend group we are with, or what family members we are talking to? Is our faith dependent on the setting we are in? How can we grow in a deeper faith this week?

☐ 5. What are the ways that God has commanded us to worship him? How can we better prepare our hearts each Sunday to properly worship him? How can we make Sunday a true Sabbath day of rest? Are there sacrifices we need to make to keep Sunday holy?

Weekly Challenge
Pray for your parish priest every day this week. If appropriate and possible, invite him over for a house blessing and meal with your family or with a small group.

Group Activity
Make a "Surrender List" with your group. Invite each person to write down five people, situations, or things in their life to surrender to God. If comfortable, go around the group and give each person an opportunity to pray out loud, surrendering these things to God.

Note of Hope

The Ark of the Covenant reminds us that God is always with us, and we are his people. We are blessed to be able to receive him and adore him in the Eucharist and dwell in his presence in a unique way. When we do, we ourselves become little tabernacles for the world, bringing Christ to all we encounter. May the light of Christ shine brightly in us, always.

SCRIPTURE VERSE TO REMEMBER

"You shall not take vengeance or bear any grudge against the sons of your own people, but you shall love your neighbor as yourself: I am the Lord."
LEVITICUS 19:18

Prayer Intentions

Response (R): Lord, we surrender all to you.
Our past, present, and future: *R.*
Our health: *R.*
Our family: *R.*
Our friends: *R.*
Our finances: *R.*
Our work: *R.*
Our suffering: *R.*
Our joys: *R.*
Our indifference: *R.*
Our passions, hobbies, and goals: *R.*
This year spent with your Word: *R.*

Our Lady of Lourdes, pray for us and all in need, especially for the sick.
Feast Day: February 11

Catechism Connection

These paragraphs in the *Catechism* may be helpful for reflection on the Scripture read this week in *The Bible in a Year*: CCC 1547, 2112, 2577

Highlight from the *Catechism*:

- "While the common priesthood of the faithful is exercised by the unfolding of baptismal grace—a life of faith, hope, and charity, a life according to the Spirit—the ministerial priesthood is at the service of the common priesthood. It is directed at the unfolding of the baptismal grace of all Christians. The ministerial priesthood is a *means* by which Christ unceasingly builds up and leads his Church. For this reason it is transmitted by its own sacrament, the sacrament of Holy Orders" (CCC 1547).

Closing Prayer

Father in heaven, we give you praise and thank you so much for your Word. Lord God, when we hear about slavery, when we hear about these things that have been such a scourge on humanity for so many years, we just ask that you enlighten our minds to be able to understand what it is that you're teaching us in allowing this to be a part of the life of the people of Israel, your people. Lord God, help us not to harden our hearts with cynicism, skepticism, or distrust but to open our hearts and minds to trusting you. We make this prayer in Jesus' name. Amen.

Opening Prayer

Father in heaven, we thank you so much for your commandments. We ask that you please be with us in all of our moments: our moments of darkness, moments of light, moments we turn away from you, and moments when we find ourselves deep in your most Sacred Heart. We make this prayer, Father, in the name of your only begotten Son, Jesus Christ our Lord, and the power of the Holy Spirit. Amen.

Reflection with Scripture

☐ 1. The book of Exodus ends with a focus on the glory of the Lord filling the Tabernacle: the worship of God. Is our end goal worship of God? How can we make our daily lives, from morning to evening, culminate in our worship of God?

☐ 2. As we begin the book of Deuteronomy, we are reminded that God gives us commandments as a mercy. His laws are laws of love. In our own leadership roles, whether in family life, volunteering, business, or elsewhere, how can we better lead with love and mercy?

☐ 3. It is traditionally said that Jesus prayed Psalm 88 when abandoned by his friends during his Passion. It is the only psalm that ends with "darkness." Jesus himself intimately knows the pain we experience. Is there something or someone causing me pain that I am avoiding acknowledging?

☐ 4. In Numbers 4, we hear how Aaron and his sons, as priests, were each assigned to do unique services and tasks. Each of us is called by God to do a unique task for the building up of his kingdom, for his glorification, and for our sanctification. What is your unique task? What is your role within your vocation?

☐ 5. In Deuteronomy, we hear the phrase "face to face" used to describe speaking to God in a deep, personal, intimate way. Do you speak intimately to God "face to face"? Do you see him as your greatest love? Someone with whom you want to grow in a deep relationship?

Weekly Challenge
Find your favorite image of Jesus, Mother Mary, the saints, or the angels, and take time to contemplate the beauty of it. How does this image bring you closer to God? What emotions does this image evoke? Is there anything new you notice in the image that you haven't noticed before? Why is this image so special to you, and why do you think you are drawn to it?

Group Activity
Invite each group member, if comfortable, to share briefly his or her vocation discernment story. Ask: How did you discern God's path for your life? Was there anyone who was particularly instrumental in your decision? If there are people in the group who are currently discerning their vocation, invite them to share any struggles they are experiencing in their discernment, along with any joys and insights they have discovered. End the discussion in prayer for those discerning, and for all vocations.

Note of Hope

The communion of saints shows us that there are many ways to live out our mission from God. From the silent prayers recited in the hiddenness of a cloister to the activity of a father who commutes an hour to work each morning, God's plan for you is unique. Of course, there is a beautiful paradox, too. Coupled with our unique mission is God's universal mission—the mission that unites each of us to all of his saints and to the very Heart of God. Each of our unique missions comes together to build up the Church for his greater glory and our holiness. May we always say "yes" just as Mary, the Queen of All Saints, did to his unique plan for us.

SCRIPTURE VERSE TO REMEMBER

*"For the LORD your God is a merciful God;
he will not fail you or destroy you or forget the covenant
with your fathers which he swore to them."*
DEUTERONOMY 4:31

Prayer Intentions

Response (R): O Lord, fill our hearts with your love.
When we worship you: *R.*
When we are working and when we are at rest: *R.*
In our prayer: *R.*
In the building up of the Church: *R.*
In our unique roles and vocations :*R.*
In our volunteer work and our ministries: *R.*
In our families: *R.*
With our friends: *R.*
During this year spent with your Word: *R.*

Catechism Connection

These paragraphs in the *Catechism* may be helpful for reflection on the Scripture read this week in *The Bible in a Year*: CCC 947, 1177, 2586

Highlights from the *Catechism*:

- "The riches of Christ are communicated to all the members, through the sacraments" (CCC 947).
- "Prayed by Christ and fulfilled in him, the Psalms remain essential to the prayer of the Church" (CCC 2586).

Closing Prayer

Father, we make this prayer of Psalm 88, and we know that you are near us in darkness. You are near us when we are alone, lonely, and isolated, and this is your prayer that you have placed in our mouths. This psalm was prayed, tradition says, by Jesus himself when he was abandoned by his friends before he was handed over to be condemned falsely. And so we know that when we are in darkness, we are not alone because you have made the darkness your home in the abandonment and the rejection of your Son, Jesus. Lord God, help us in darkness to see your face and know that you're present. Help us always to have confidence in you. We make this prayer in the name of Jesus, the One who entered into darkness for our sake. Amen.

Opening Prayer

Father in heaven, you are good, and you protect us. You bear us up as on the wings of eagles, lest we dash our foot against a stone. Yet, Lord God, every day we are tried, and life reveals the truth of our fickle, shaky, and quick-to-forget hearts. Lord, help us to never forget what you have done for us. In Jesus' name, we pray. Amen.

Reflection with Scripture

☐ 1. Fr. Mike explains that much of the Nazarite vow in Numbers 6 is dedicating time to the Lord. What parts of our day do we dedicate to the Lord? How can we steward our time in a better way each day?

☐ 2. As we read through the Ten Commandments, Fr. Mike reminds us that the reason for the rules is relationship. Without the relationship, he says, those rules can be hollow and empty. This is seen in a powerful way later in the New Testament when Jesus says, "If you love me, you will keep my commandments" (John 14:15). What do God's commandments reveal about his love for us? And how can we respond in a relationship of love instead of seeing his commands as a list of rules to follow?

☐ 3. In Deuteronomy 7, we hear God tell his people that they are chosen because of his love and mercy, not because they have done anything to earn his choice. In a world that tells us we have to work hard to earn and prove ourselves, have we let the lie enter our hearts that God only loves us for what we do instead of for who we are? How can we live in the reality of his love, recognizing that we are loved into being as his chosen people?

☐ 4. In Deuteronomy 8, the Israelites are forewarned that they will experience such abundant blessings from God that they need to stand strong against their temptations to forget the Lord in their abundance. How can we, too, stand firm when facing this same temptation?

☐ 5. In Psalm 33:11, we hear, "The counsel of the LORD stands for ever." Do I go first to God when I need counsel? Or do I place more importance and weight in other people's opinions than God's wisdom, direction, and counsel for my life?

Weekly Challenge

Take time this week to remember someone who has influenced your prayer life. Write them a thank you note, email, or text, naming ways he or she has helped you grow in your faith and prayer. As you write and send the note, offer a prayer in thanksgiving.

Group Activity

Discuss as a group one thing that all the members can sacrifice this coming week to offer to the Lord, to grow in self-control, self-discipline, and temperance. Ideas for sacrifice: favorite TV show, social media use, cream and sugar in daily coffee, meat two times during the week, etc. Replace the thing sacrificed with daily Mass, extra prayer time, or a work of charity.

Note of Hope

We must make time each day to arrange our day around prayer: a simple morning offering when we awake, a look of gratitude toward heaven throughout our work day, marking ourselves and our loved ones with the Sign of the Cross, a Holy Hour spent in Adoration, Bible study, the Liturgy of the Hours, the Rosary, or Mass. Prayer is necessary for our soul's flourishing and unites us to God, the heavenly hosts, and the rest of humanity. Everything hinges on our relationship with Christ, and prayer allows Christ, who is Merciful Love, to reign in our hearts. This week, let us remember: prayer brings us into relationship with our Creator, the One we love, our best and closest friend.

SCRIPTURE VERSE TO REMEMBER

"For you are a people holy to the Lord your God; the Lord your God has chosen you to be a people for his own possession, out of all the peoples that are on the face of the earth."
DEUTERONOMY 7:6

Prayer Intentions

Response (R): O Lord, bless us and keep us.
When we are tempted to disobey: *R.*
When we are tempted to forget the Lord in our abundance: *R.*
During seasons of difficulty: *R.*
In our lack of self-discipline and self-control: *R.*
In the abundance of your forgiveness and mercy: *R.*
As we yearn for a greater relationship with you: *R.*
In both the ordinary and the extraordinary moments: *R.*
During this year spent in your Word: *R.*

Catechism Connection

These paragraphs in the *Catechism* may be helpful for reflection on the Scripture read this week in *The Bible in a Year*: CCC 916, 1809, 1834

St. Gabriel of Our Lady of Sorrows, pray for us and all in need, especially Catholic youth, students, and seminarians.
Feast Day: February 27

Highlight from the *Catechism*:

- "The human virtues are stable dispositions of the intellect and the will that govern our acts, order our passions, and guide our conduct in accordance with reason and faith. They can be grouped around the four cardinal virtues: prudence, justice, fortitude, and temperance" (CCC 1834).

Closing Prayer

Father in heaven, we thank you that when we are unfaithful, you remain faithful. That is what we need. You are who we need because the depth to which our fears and lack of faith can control us is paralyzing at times. And yet, Lord, when we know who you are and love you, that perfect love casts out whatever fear we might experience. Lord, if our day today is marked with fear, we ask that you please place your love in our hearts. If our day today is marked with uncertainty and insecurity, we ask that you place your courage and strength in our hearts. Lord God, above all, we ask that you place us in the palm of your hand and help us never to run away. In Jesus' name, we pray. Amen.

Opening Prayer

Father in heaven, we thank you for your Word. For the times we feel perplexed or troubled by it, we ask you to replace our skepticism or cynicism with a spirit of openness, truth, and honesty. Lord God, give us a spirit of trust that is open to whatever you will for us. In Jesus' name, we pray. Amen.

Reflection with Scripture

☐ 1. In Psalm 96:9 we hear: "Worship the LORD in holy attire." How can we make an extra effort on Sundays to honor the Lord in what we wear, how we carry ourselves, and how we prepare and present our hearts to the Lord in worship?

☐ 2. We hear in Deuteronomy 14 the instructions for how God wanted his people to tithe. It is one of the precepts of the Church to contribute according to our means to the support of the Church. What are the spiritual benefits of tithing? How much of my resources do I give the Lord? How can I cultivate an attitude of generosity?

☐ 3. In Numbers 16, Korah, Dathan, and Abiram rebel against Moses and Aaron, inquiring, "Why then do you exalt yourselves above the assembly of the LORD?" (Numbers 16:3). When I see holiness in others, especially people who are in leadership roles in our Church, does my spirit rebel against them? Or do I rejoice in others' talents, gifts, and holiness? How can I shift my mindset from one of rebellion to gratitude?

□ 4. In Deuteronomy 17:3, God instructs his people not to serve any "other gods … or the sun or the moon or any of the host of heaven." And in Deuteronomy 18, we hear all forms of divination should be rejected. How can we more fully place our trust in God, knowing that he has given us free will to make choices and that we must take that responsibility?

□ 5. At the end of Deuteronomy 21, we hear "if a man … is put to death and you hang him on a tree, his body shall not remain all night upon the tree, but you shall bury him the same day, for a hanged man is accursed by God" (Deuteronomy 21:23). These verses prefigure Christ's death in a powerful way. What are some ways we can contemplate Jesus' willingness to suffer and die for us so that we may live?

Weekly Challenge

Each evening this week, reflect on your interactions with others. Did you live out God's Great Commandment to love him with your whole strength and to love your neighbor as yourself? End with an act of contrition and a prayer, asking God for the grace of an increase in love of our neighbors.

Group Activity

Read and discuss the greatest commandments in Matthew 22:37–39: What does loving the Lord with all our heart, soul, and mind look like? Brainstorm some ways to live out these two commandments this week.

Note of Hope

When the Israelites rebel and lose faith, God sends serpents that bite the people so that "many sons of Israel died" (Numbers 21:6). God instructed Moses to set up a bronze serpent so that when people gazed at it, they would live. This all points to the Cross: The sign of shame becomes our sign of hope in Jesus. We know we can boast in our weakness, knowing that when we unite our shame, anxiety, and fears to the Cross of Christ, he will transform us in the hope of his Resurrection. May we never be too ashamed to bring our weaknesses to the transforming Cross of love, where our King and Savior of mercy reigns.

SCRIPTURE VERSE TO REMEMBER

*"For the LORD is good; his mercy endures for ever,
and his faithfulness to all generations."*
PSALM 100:5

Prayer Intentions

Response (R): Give us the hope of the Resurrection, O Lord!
May our Church unite in the mission to spread the Good News to the ends of the earth: **R.**
For those who have never heard your Name spoken: **R.**
For those who turn to divination instead of the wisdom of your Cross: **R.**
For all teachers of our Faith: **R.**
For our leaders: **R.**
For our country and for the world: **R.**
For the graces and blessings prepared for us this year through your Word: **R.**

St. Katharine Drexel, pray for us and all in need, especially those seeking racial justice.
Feast Day: March 3

Catechism Connection

These paragraphs in the *Catechism* may be helpful for reflection on the Scripture read this week in *The Bible in a Year*: CCC 618, 1962, 2116

Highlights from the *Catechism*:

- "Apart from the cross there is no other ladder by which we may get to heaven" (CCC 618).
- "The Decalogue is a light offered to the conscience of every man to make God's call and ways known to him and to protect him against evil" (CCC 1962).

Closing Prayer

Father in heaven, we give you praise, and we thank you. We thank you for your Word. We thank you for loving us. We thank you for choosing us. We thank you for showing us your heart, the heart of a Father who loves his children. In the midst of this day, Lord, we call upon your name, and we ask you, Father, to send us your Holy Spirit, in the name of your Son Jesus Christ. As you receive our thanks, and as you receive our praise, in Jesus' name, we ask you also to send your Spirit upon us. Amen.

Opening Prayer

Father in heaven, we thank you for Psalm 106, which reminds us to remember all you have done, your faithfulness, and all the ways in which we have failed to belong to you. Lord God, today, please call us back to yourself and give us a spirit of repentance, trust, and confidence in your mercy for us. Lord, give us your Holy Spirit so that we may be your people this and every day. In Jesus' name, we pray. Amen.

Reflection with Scripture

☐ 1. Though many of the laws of Deuteronomy seem arbitrary at first glance, when we look more deeply, we see that it might not be what we anticipate, but it is what we need. How can we connect this to how we live out God's commands? Do we see him as the provider for all our needs?

☐ 2. Balaam was hired to curse, yet God intervenes. Instead of a curse, Balaam speaks words of blessing over Israel. What does this teach us about how God can use any person he desires, even those outside of the Faith or whose intentions are not pure, to accomplish his plans? What does this tell us about God's sovereignty and power?

☐ 3. Numbers recounts the narrative of the Israelites getting closer to the end of their Desert Wanderings. During this time, as they struggled with trust in the Lord's goodness and providence, God was purifying, testing, and disciplining his people. Through it all, he showed them great patience and deep mercy. During times of dryness, like a spiritual desert in our own lives, what can we learn from the Israelites? How can their mistakes and their triumphs teach us? How does God show us patience and gentleness?

☐ 4. His relationship with Moses helped Joshua prepare to be Moses' successor. Moses mentored him for years, teaching him through his own example. Who are your mentors? Who do you look up to in the Faith? Who can you learn and grow from?

☐ 5. In Deuteronomy 30:19, we hear God's call and invitation to "choose life." What spiritual and lifestyle changes do we need to make to ensure we are choosing life? What acts of darkness, sloth, and sin that lead to spiritual death do we need to stop?

Weekly Challenge

This week, take note of the relationships, activities, hobbies, habits, and things that are not helping you grow closer to God. These are things that are hindering you from choosing life. How can you transform these things into what is life-giving? Are there things you need to stop doing completely? Ask God for the grace and courage to make these changes.

Group Activity

Take time to talk about the greatest leaders you have encountered in your life. Write down the qualities and virtues that make a good, strong leader, and invite each group member to share. End the discussion with a prayer for leaders, especially the pope, bishops, and priests.

Note of Hope

The Lord invites us each day to "choose life!" May we always remember that he is the Way, the Truth, and the Life, without whom we can do nothing. God desires us to live a life of abundance in him (see John 10:10). In his tender compassion and mercy for us, he bestows on us grace upon grace. He shows us the path that leads to life through his own witness of love and sacrifice, his commandments, and his friends, the saints. May we be counted among them.

SCRIPTURE VERSE TO REMEMBER

"And if you obey the voice of the LORD your God, being careful to do all his commandments which I command you this day, the LORD your God will set you high above all the nations of the earth."
DEUTERONOMY 28:1

Prayer Intentions

Response (R): Lord, grant life in you.

For our brothers and sisters in war-torn areas of the world: **R.**

For our brothers and sisters who are experiencing disease and famine: **R.**

For our brothers and sisters who are displaced and do not know where to turn: **R.**

For our brothers and sisters who are unemployed and searching for work: **R.**

For our brothers and sisters experiencing financial trouble: **R.**

For our brothers and sisters who are homeless and hungry: **R.**

For us, in this year spent with your Word: **R.**

St. Francis of Rome, patron saint of motorists and widows, pray for us.
Feast Day: March 9

Catechism Connection

These paragraphs in the *Catechism* may be helpful for reflection on the Scripture read this week in *The Bible in a Year*: CCC 1446, 1450, 1964

Highlight from the *Catechism*:

- "Christ instituted the Sacrament of Penance for all sinful members of his Church: above all for those who, since Baptism, have fallen into grave sin, and have thus lost their baptismal grace and wounded ecclesial communion" (CCC 1446).

Closing Prayer

Father in heaven, we lift up our voices and hearts to you. We know that you are the Lord. You are God, and you are good, and you call us to be yours even though you know our weakness and our frailty—even though you know that we will turn away from you. You still fight for us and call us to belong to you. You still love us even in the midst of our faithlessness. You love us when we do not love you. You are good, you are God, and we give you praise. Today, help us in our weakness. When we have failed, remind us of your faithfulness so that we can turn back to you, call upon your mercy and grace, and be restored by your love. We make this prayer in the mighty name of Jesus Christ our Lord. Amen.

Opening Prayer

Father in heaven, we give you praise. Your mercy endures forever. We love you for that. We love you for who you are. We love you for all your blessings. We love you for your true fatherhood. Help us to be true sons and daughters of such a good father. We make this prayer in Jesus' name. Amen.

Reflection with Scripture

☐ 1. The Promised Land was a geographical area given to the Israelites at a time in history. Yet we can also see it as a spiritual metaphor as we journey here on earth toward our heavenly home. Jesus tells us that the Kingdom of God begins here on earth. How can we dwell in this "promised land" right now, in the present moment?

☐ 2. Reflecting on the ending of the book of Numbers, Fr. Mike reminds us that we are not meant to live alone in the world; rather, we are connected to others. We are made for both community and communion. Is there someone you know who is in need of greater community? How can you help that person? Is there a ministry you can invite him or her to join? A person you can introduce?

☐ 3. What did the Lord teach you through the books of Numbers and Deuteronomy? What is your greatest takeaway from them?

☐ 4. To conquer Jericho, the Israelites obey God's plan by walking around the city for seven days in a liturgical procession and then blowing their trumpets and shouting on the seventh day. In the midst of our own battles, is our plan to praise and worship God? What can we learn from this story?

☐ 5. Joshua's bold prayer that God make the sun stay still in the midst of the battle shows his complete trust in God. St. Teresa of Avila said that we pay God a compliment when we ask big things of him. It shows that we know he is all-powerful. Is there a "big" intention that you want to ask God? Do you feel like you can fully entrust this intention to him?

Weekly Challenge

This week, make sure to speak of the Lord's goodness to others and the way he is working in your life. Pray for the opportunities for these conversations and the courage to speak about him to others. If someone asks more about God, invite that person to pray with you or to come to an event at your parish.

Group Activity

As a group, go for a "Walls of Jericho" prayer walk. Begin by offering up your intentions together to God and then pray a Chaplet of Divine Mercy together as a group as you walk. If weather or physical disabilities make it impossible to walk, pray together in a designated place, offering up your intentions to God.

Note of Hope

God blesses our obedience and boldness of heart. He desires us to break down the walls of fear, anxiety, and anger so that our hearts, minds, and relationships may be free to do his will. We are created for community and communion with him and his people. This week, may we see Christ in all we encounter, and may we proclaim him to all we meet.

SCRIPTURE VERSE TO REMEMBER

"Have I not commanded you? Be strong and of good courage; be not frightened, neither be dismayed; for the LORD your God is with you wherever you go."
DEUTERONOMY 28:1

Prayer Intentions

Response (R): Lord, you do not fail or forsake us.

When we fight our battles each day: **R.**

When we spread your name: **R.**

When we serve those in need: **R.**

When we are lonely: **R.**

In trials and seasons of dryness: **R.**

In our sinfulness: **R.**

In our return to you: **R.**

In all things: **R.**

In this year spent with your Word: **R.**

Catechism Connection

These paragraphs in the *Catechism* may be helpful for reflection on the Scripture read this week in *The Bible in a Year*: CCC 162, 302, 2090

St. Joseph, pray for us and all in need, especially the Universal Church, families, fathers, expectant mothers, travelers, immigrants, house sellers and buyers, craftsmen, engineers, and workers.
Feast Day: March 19

Highlight from the *Catechism*:

- "Hope is the confident expectation of divine blessing and the beatific vision of God; it is also the fear of offending God's love and of incurring punishment" (CCC 2090).

Closing Prayer

Father in heaven, we know that you have revealed yourself to us, and so we thank you. We know that you have revealed that you desire justice. You desire peace. You are the God of peace. In fact, you revealed that Jesus is the Prince of Peace. And yet, when we hear so many stories of war and of battle and of violence, it can cause us to question. So we ask you, Lord, please give us interior peace. Give us a sense of understanding of what you want to teach us today and what you want us to receive today. We make this prayer in the name of the Prince of Peace, in the name of Jesus Christ our Lord. Amen.

Opening Prayer

Father in heaven, we thank you for bringing us all the way through the Bible, your Word, to this point. And we know that without your Word, we would not even know who you are. We can see your fingerprints in the world around us. We can see hints at your truth in the world you created, as we can see the person of the artist in the artwork. Yet, Lord, we still might not know your heart unless you revealed your heart to us. And so we ask you to please continue to reveal your heart to us so that we can reveal our hearts to you. In Jesus' name, we pray. Amen.

Reflection with Scripture

☐ 1. Joshua 13 begins with God telling Joshua, "You are old and advanced in years, and there remains yet very much land to be possessed." Whether we are old or young, what are some ways that we can stay childlike in our faith, completing God's mission for our lives with verve and joy?

☐ 2. God's will is that his people, the Israelites, may be at peace, in union, and reconciled with all nations. Yet even more, he desires them to be in union with him. How can we keep this at the forefront of our hearts and minds as we hear about the battles and the destruction that are so prevalent in the book of Joshua? How can we see this as part of God's redemptive plan for his people?

☐ 3. At the end of Joshua 21, we hear the fulfillment of the Lord's promise. Can you share a personal story of when God's promise to you was fulfilled in your life?

☐ 4. What qualities can we imitate in Deborah in her role as a judge?

☐ 5. How does Ruth's relationship with Naomi, her mother-in-law, reflect the covenantal relationship God made with his people?

Weekly Challenge

This week, reflect on Joshua's proclamation of faithfulness to God. How can you imprint this message spiritually in the heart of your home? Reflect on your family or community. How is God asking you and your family or community to serve the Lord? Is it through hospitality? Cooking meals for families in need? Making peace within your family? Being a witness of hope to others? Ask the Holy Spirit to reveal to you how he is calling you to serve.

Group Activity

Ask each group member to write down on a small piece of paper one concrete way that he or she serves his or her family. Fold up the papers, put them into a bowl or bag, and mix them up. Have each member pick out a piece of paper, silently read the act of service that is written on it, and consider doing that act of service in the coming week.

Note of Hope

Joshua was a strong leader who loved the Lord and his people. He was an instrument in God's plan for peace and prosperity, and through his suffering and battles, he helped bring God's people into freedom. God sent us an even stronger leader in Jesus, his dearly beloved Son, who is Peace himself. We are able to approach him, the fount of forgiveness and mercy, with confidence, knowing that he will fight our battles with and for us. This week, may we remember that he is always with us.

SCRIPTURE VERSE TO REMEMBER

"O Israel, hope in the LORD! For with the LORD there is mercy, and with him is plenteous redemption."
PSALM 130:7

Prayer Intentions

Response (R): As for me, I will serve the Lord.
When I don't understand why a situation is happening: *R.*
When I am confused and disheartened: *R.*
When I am filled with joy and peace: *R.*
When I want to be instantly gratified: *R.*
When I disagree with others: *R.*
When I work toward peace: *R.*
When I seek reconciliation and healing: *R.*
In this year spent with your Word: *R.*

St. Turibius of Mogrovejo, pray for us and all in need, especially for native peoples and for the bishops in Latin America.
Feast Day: March 23

Catechism Connection

These paragraphs in the *Catechism* may be helpful for reflection on the Scripture read this week in *The Bible in a Year*: CCC 2096, 2639, 2712

Highlight from the *Catechism*:

- "Adoration is the first act of the virtue of religion. To adore God is to acknowledge him as God, as the Creator and Savior, the Lord and Master of everything that exists, as infinite and merciful Love" (CCC 2096).

Closing Prayer

Father in heaven, may your name be praised. May your name be glorified. May we know who you are and lift up our voices and our hearts to always honor you, always praise you, and always thank you. In Jesus' name, we pray. Amen.

Opening Prayer

Father in heaven, we give you praise and glory. We give you honor, and we declare our love for you and our gratitude for who you are and all you have given to us this day and every day. In Jesus' name, we pray. Amen.

Reflection with Scripture

☐ 1. The stories found within Judges often reflect a cycle within our own hearts: We turn away from God, we repent, God forgives us, and yet we turn away from him again. How can we apply these lessons we learn from Judges to our own fickle hearts?

☐ 2. In Judges, we read about Samson, who reminds us that though we may appear strong, there are weak areas in our lives. Do we give the Lord permission each day to work in our hearts and heal us of our weaknesses? Do we desire this healing?

☐ 3. Samson continuously placed himself in situations of temptation. Do I do the same? If so, what are the ways I can stop?

☐ 4. The book of Judges ends with a horrific story. Although God's Chosen People should have been the first to uphold the sacredness of the human person and the human body, instead, the corruption of sin is seen. Is purity of heart something that I desire? Do I pray for it daily? What changes can I make to seek out pure and true love?

☐ 5. Judges ends with the words: "Every man did what was right in his own eyes" (Judges 21:25). We, too, live in an age of relativism. Are we afraid to proclaim objective truth to others? How can we explain objective truth to others who inquire about it?

Weekly Challenge

Each day this week, offer a Glory Be for couples experiencing loss and infertility. If you feel called, reach out to a couple you know who is experiencing this suffering and tell them you are praying for them. Ask them if they have any prayer intentions. Invite them over for coffee or a meal, or to go to church and pray together.

Group Activity

Samson was known for his physical strength, but he did not show strength of soul. While physical strength is a gift, even more vital is strength of character and will, which is called virtue. The four "cardinal virtues," which are the basis of many others, are prudence, justice, fortitude, and temperance. As a group, look up these virtues in the *Catechism* (CCC 1833–1838) and discuss how to apply them to daily life. How does knowing both your strengths and weaknesses help in building up your own character as well as God's kingdom?

Note of Hope

During Christ's Passion, Pontius Pilate asks of him, "What is truth?" (John 18:38). We hear in the book of Judges that "every man did what was right in his own eyes" (Judges 21:25), meaning each person acted as if he had his own "truths." Yet we know that Jesus is the Way, the Truth, and the Life. We know that he brings meaning into our lives and that all truth comes from him. We know that we can trust in his truth and that his truth is good for us. May we yearn for and learn from his truth each day.

SCRIPTURE VERSE TO REMEMBER

"There is none holy like the Lord,
there is none besides you; there is no rock like our God."
PSALM 130:7

Prayer Intentions

Response (R): Have mercy on us, Lord, our Redeemer.
When we are stuck in a cycle of sin: *R.*
When we doubt your goodness: *R.*
When we sin recklessly: *R.*
When we don't live out our vocations: *R.*
When we choose relativism instead of your objective truth: *R.*
When we are not pure of heart: *R.*
When we are imprudent in speech: *R.*
In this year spent with you in your Word: *R.*

Catechism Connection

These paragraphs in the *Catechism* may be helpful for reflection on the Scripture read this week in *The Bible in a Year*: CCC 303, 2574, 2443, 2738

Highlight from the *Catechism*:

* "God cares for all, from the least things to the great events of the world and its history" (CCC 303).

Closing Prayer

Father in heaven, you are our helper. You are our comforter, and Lord God, you are also our vindicator. You are the One who rises up and makes us righteous. It is not our own works, Lord God, that make us righteous in your sight. It is you. It is your grace that you have given to us, that you won on the Cross. You handed yourself over for us, Lord God. You made it possible for us to experience your mercy, to have access to the heart of the Father, and to be able to receive the Holy Spirit deep in our hearts. So we ask you, Father in heaven, in the name of your Son, Jesus Christ, renew your Holy Spirit in our lives so that everything we do may begin with your inspiration and be carried out by your saving and loving help to its completion, which gives you glory. In Jesus' name, we pray. Amen.

Opening Prayer

Father in heaven, you so loved the world that you gave your only beloved Son, so that we would not have to die, but so that we could have life. So that we could have you. So that we can know that you know us and that we matter to you. We are so grateful. Help us to receive this gift with everything we are and everything we have. In Jesus' name, we pray. Amen.

Reflection with Scripture

☐ 1. Jesus asks the first disciples, "What do you seek?" (John 1:38). Jesus asks each of us the same question: "What do we seek?" What is the most important reality in my life? What drives me? What am I seeking in this life?

☐ 2. In John 5, we hear Jesus ask the man who had been ill for thirty-eight years if he wants to be healed. Do I truly desire spiritual, physical, mental, and emotional healing, or does the thought of healing frighten me? Am I doing all I can to heal, or have I grown weary in seeking healing?

☐ 3. In John 6, we hear that Jesus proclaimed the reality of the Eucharist, but many of his listeners did not accept his words. How can we live out our belief that the Eucharist is truly the Body, Blood, Soul, and Divinity of Jesus? How can we bring this truth to others?

☐ 4. During his suffering on the Cross, Jesus entrusts his Mother to St. John and, in doing so, to all disciples. Do we see Mother

Mary as our spiritual mother? How can we grow in a deeper relationship with Our Lady?

☐ 5. St. Peter returned to his boat and fishing after Jesus' Resurrection. When I am tired and lonely, do I turn to Christ or to worldly comforts? Are there steps I can take when I am depleted to turn to God (for example, writing a letter instead of scrolling through social media)?

Weekly Challenge
This week, choose a favorite verse from the Gospel of John and repeat it each day. Write it down or try to memorize it. Reflect on why this verse caught your attention and how you can let the words penetrate your life.

Group Activity
Pick one weekday this week to attend daily Mass together. If your schedule does not permit this, invite group members to choose a day to make a spiritual communion and remember each other in their intentions.

Spiritual Communion Prayer
My Jesus, I believe that you are present in the Most Holy Sacrament. I love you above all things, and I desire to receive you into my soul. Since I cannot at this moment receive you sacramentally, come at least spiritually into my heart. I embrace you as if you were already there and unite myself wholly to you. Never permit me to be separated from you. Amen.

Note of Hope

Jesus gave us a "new commandment" at the Last Supper. On the same day he instituted the Eucharist, he instructed us, "Love one another; even as I have loved you" (John 13:34). St. Thérèse of Lisieux responded to this commandment in her autobiography, *Story of a Soul*, writing,

> Lord, I know You don't command the impossible. You know better than I do my weakness and imperfection; You know very well that never would I be able to love my Sisters as You love them, unless *You*, O my Jesus, *loved them in me*. It is because You wanted to give me this grace that You made Your new commandment. Oh! How I love this new commandment since it gives me the assurance that Your Will is *to love in me* all those You command me to love. Yes, I feel it, when I am charitable, it is Jesus alone who is acting in me, and the more united I am to him, the more also do I love my sisters.[4]

Let us always realize the truth in this Doctor of the Church's words: that Jesus does not command the impossible. When we are tempted to love people less than we should, may we always turn to Jesus and ask him to love them in and through us, knowing that with him, all things are possible (see Luke 1:37).

SCRIPTURE VERSE TO REMEMBER

"And the Word became flesh and dwelt among us, full of grace and truth; we have beheld his glory, glory as of the only-begotten Son from the Father."
JOHN 1:14

---

4. Thérèse of Lisieux, *Story of a Soul* (West Chester, PA: Ascension, 2024), 287, original emphasis.

Prayer Intentions

St. John Baptist de la Salle, pray for us all, especially for teachers and students.
Feast Day: April 7

Response (R): Jesus, you who are the Word made Flesh, dwell among us!
In life's challenges: *R.*
As we proclaim you as Lord: *R.*
When we testify to your Truth: *R.*
As we live out your New Commandment to love as you love: *R.*
In the reception of the Eucharist: *R.*
As we adore you, present in the Eucharist: *R.*
When we ask your Mother's intercession: *R.*
In this year spent with your Word: *R.*

Catechism Connection

These paragraphs in the *Catechism* may be helpful for reflection on the Scripture read this week in *The Bible in a Year*: CCC 654, 1392, 1823, 2466

Highlight from the *Catechism*:

- "The Paschal mystery has two aspects: by his death, Christ liberates us from sin; by his Resurrection, he opens for us the way to a new life" (CCC 654).

Closing Prayer

Father in heaven, we thank you. Thank you so much not only for the gift of the sacrifice of your Son, who laid down his life. It was not taken from him; he laid it down of his own accord. Thank you so much for the gift of your Son, who came into this world not to condemn the world but to save the world. He appeared to the disciples, speaking that powerful word *shalom*, the powerful word "peace." Peace which the world cannot give he has given to us, as he gave to the disciples the ability to forgive sins, the restoration of the kingdom, and his Holy Spirit that dwells inside of us. In Jesus' name, we thank you. Amen.

Opening Prayer

Father in heaven, we give you praise and thanks. Thank you for this day. Thank you for leading us by your Spirit to hear your Word once again, to go into this new stage of the Royal Kingdom, and to see the beginnings of how you not only blessed the twelve tribes of Israel but also brought them together. And you brought them together into a Royal Kingdom in order to bless us. You have done this in order to prefigure the Church that you founded in Jesus Christ. You gave us your Holy Spirit, that same Spirit that came upon Saul, son of Kish, to lead him and to guide him, so he could be a prophet and king; so he could lead; so he could fight the enemies of the people of Israel and unite the people of Israel. You have given us your same Holy Spirit. So, right now, Lord, we just give you thanks, and we ask you, please renew the gift of your Spirit in each one of us. Let us always say yes to you in everything that we are and everything that we do. In Jesus' name, we pray. Amen.

Reflection with Scripture

☐ 1. Saul is given the spiritual gifts and graces he needs to accomplish his role and vocation as king. In what ways have you experienced God's graces to live out your vocation?

☐ 2. Instead of killing the people he conquered, Saul let them go and offered a peace offering before the Lord and "rejoiced greatly" (1 Samuel 11:15). Is there someone in my life that I can show mercy to right now? Who is the first person that comes to mind when I read this? How would my life change if I extended peace to that person?

☐ 3. Often, God cooperates with our hardness of heart because of the greatness, patience, and mercy of his own Heart. How can we grow in devotion to his Sacred Heart? How can we imitate his merciful Heart in our love of others who have hardened their hearts against us?

☐ 4. David was prepared to battle Goliath because he had not avoided the smaller battles in his life. What are our daily "battles"? Why might we feel tempted to avoid our daily duties, the everyday tasks that God is calling for us to do within our vocation? How can we face our battles today so we can conquer the giants of tomorrow?

☐ 5. In 1 Samuel 18, we hear how Jonathan loved David as his friend. Who are your closest friends? What virtues do they excel in? How have they led you closer to God?

Weekly Challenge

This week, pick something to do one day to combat the sin of vanity, which is the inordinate focus on what others think of us. Some ideas include: choosing not to wear makeup, avoiding making comments on social media, or listening to others completely as they speak instead of thinking of what to say next.

Group Activity

As a group, watch Fr. Mike's video "The Symptoms of Vanity (and the Surprising Cure)," available for free on the Ascension Presents YouTube channel. Discuss what Fr. Mike says, as well as what you can change and implement in your life to combat this deadly sin.

Note of Hope

When our hearts are troubled, hardened, or weary, God's Heart is always ready to comfort ours and fill it with himself. There is no heart too hardened for him to heal. May we know that he is always waiting for us and ready to give us himself, even and especially within the moments that we feel weak. May we always have the childlike courage to say yes to our Father's love for us!

SCRIPTURE VERSE TO REMEMBER

"If you will fear the LORD and serve him and listen to his voice and not rebel against the commandment of the LORD, and if both you and the king who reigns over you will follow the LORD your God, it will be well."
1 SAMUEL 12:14

Prayer Intentions

Response (R): Lord, send us your Spirit.
As we fight our daily battles: *R.*
In living out the duties of our vocation: *R.*
As we strive to be a virtuous friend: *R.*
For the grace to combat our vanity: *R.*
As we keep our mind and heart set on your plan for us: *R.*
In the reception of the graces you lavish on us: *R.*
In this year spent with your Word: *R.*

Catechism Connection

These paragraphs in the *Catechism* may be helpful for reflection on the Scripture read this week in *The Bible in a Year*: CCC 1829, 2519, 2848

Highlight from the *Catechism*:

- "The 'pure in heart' are promised that they will see God face to face and be like him. Purity of heart is the precondition of the vision of God" (CCC 2519).

Closing Prayer

Father in heaven, we give you praise and glory. Thank you for your Word, and thank you for the gift of friendship. Lord God, we see a true friendship between Jonathan and David, and we give you thanks for all the people in our lives, whether they be a few or great in number, who have been faithful to us. Thank you for the people you have brought into our lives who have cared for us, protected us, or even just done their best to be a friend. Lord God, at this moment we pray for all of them. We pray for every person who has ever loved us, even those who have not loved us like they should have. In this moment, we also lift up before you every heart that is lonely and isolated—every heart that does not know friendship. We pray for all those who feel unseen, unknown, and unloved. They are our brothers and sisters. Lord God, we pray for them in the name of your Son, Jesus Christ our Lord. Amen.

Opening Prayer

Father in heaven, we give you praise today. We know what it is like to be betrayed and lied about. We know what it is to lose faith in others when they have turned their backs on us. We know what it is to be hurt by having trusted others, having given our hearts to them, and being betrayed. And so, in David's prayer in Psalm 52, we recognize our own experience. We recognize what it is to be abandoned: to have had friends and then to have those friends turn on us. And so we pray for each other, especially those betrayed hearts, especially those who find themselves wounded by those they thought they could trust. And we ask for their strength, for grace, and for mercy to be in their hearts. In Jesus' name, we pray. Amen.

Reflection with Scripture

☐ 1. Throughout the first book of Samuel, God is continually present to his people Israel, even in the midst of their rejection, failures, and disobedience. Do I truly believe that God is ever-present with us? That he will not abandon us? That even in our sin he still calls us back to him?

☐ 2. David flees to save his life from Saul. Throughout this hardship of fearing for his life, David turned to God in prayer. How can we imitate David during times marked by difficulty and fear?

☐ 3. Saul violates the commandments of the Lord. At Nob, he puts the priests of the Lord to death for helping David, and then he consults a medium. What does this teach us about allowing our insecurities to rule over our actions? When I experience a feeling of desperation, what actionable steps can I take to turn to God in hope, trust, and faith?

☐ 4. David had a chance to kill Saul, yet he didn't, even though those around him encouraged him to. How can we discern God's will in our lives when the advice of others may conflict with his plan for us?

☐ 5. Do we worry about the future like Saul? Or do we trust in God's providence like David? How can we temper any unhealthy curiosities about the future and place our trust in God?

Weekly Challenge

We learn that David had the virtue of mercy, the virtue of reverence, and the virtue of faithfulness. How can we personally grow in these three virtues? Which one stands out the most? Each day this week, pray for an increase in these virtues.

Group Activity

If there are enough people, divide into three separate groups. The first group represents Samuel, the second Saul, and the third David. Have each group determine the most important lesson that each of these figures can teach us about how to live out our Faith. When everyone is prepared, have the groups come together and share that lesson with everyone.

Note of Hope

The Lord asks us to trust him in the present moment. He has a plan for us right now and a plan for our future. Later in Scripture, we hear Jesus instruct us not to be "anxious about tomorrow" but rather to "seek first his kingdom and his righteousness" (see Matthew 6:33–34). We can trust the Lord to take care of our past, present, and future. When we do, we are able to open the eyes of our heart to clearly seek first his kingdom.

SCRIPTURE VERSE TO REMEMBER

"The Lord is my rock, and my fortress, and my deliverer, my God, my rock, in whom I take refuge, my shield, and the horn of my salvation, my stronghold."
PSALM 18:2

Prayer Intentions

Response (R): Forgive us, Lord, as we forgive those who trespass against us.

As we approach your mercy in the confessional: **R.**

When we need the courage to extend mercy to those who have hurt us: **R.**

When we desire to seek revenge but turn to your mercy instead: **R.**

When we pray, "Blessed are the peacemakers": **R.**

When we need a deeper understanding of the reality that no sin is too big for your mercy: **R.**

In this year spent with your Word: **R.**

Catechism Connection

These paragraphs in the *Catechism* may be helpful for reflection on the Scripture read this week in *The Bible in a Year*: CCC 368, 2566, 2842

Highlight from the *Catechism*:

- "'You, therefore, must be perfect, as your heavenly Father is perfect'; 'Be merciful, even as your Father is merciful'; 'A new commandment I give to you, that you love one another, even as I have loved you, that you also love one another'" (CCC 2842).

Closing Prayer

Father in heaven, we give you praise and glory. We thank you so much for this opportunity to listen to your Word. You revealed not only the fact that you called Saul but also the way our choices, even in the midst of being called, can either raise us up to you or lead us away from you. Lord God, we ask you to please help us to be people who say yes to you—people who have been chosen by you and then are faithful to you, because every one of us has a heart like Saul. Every one of us has a heart that can turn away, and we just ask you to please always keep us near your heart and never let us wander away. Never let us die alone or apart from you, but always allow us to walk with you and to die in you. We ask this in the name of Jesus Christ our Lord. Amen.

Opening Prayer

Father in heaven, we thank you for all the unseen ways in which you have guided our lives and protected us from potential dangers. We could have been destroyed, and yet here we are today, able to listen to your Word, to receive your love, and to love you in return. Please help us to have the lens to see that no day is earned, but every day is a gift. In Jesus' name, we pray. Amen.

Reflection with Scripture

☐ 1. Instead of being held captive by the memory of Saul, David honors him by lamenting his death. This shows David's strength of character. Is there a person or situation that I am held captive by? What are some actions I can take this week to free myself from this spiritual, mental, or emotional burden?

☐ 2. With Saul's death comes a division within Israel when the southern tribe of Judah anoints David as its king and the northern tribes select Saul's son, Ish-bosheth, as king. At times, the loss of a leader or the death of a loved one can unearth division. How can we sow peace in our families and communities in times of stress?

☐ 3. As we read 2 Samuel, we encounter battles. How can I help end disagreements and fighting in my family, especially conflicts that stretch across generations? Is there a part I can play in the reconciliation and peace of my family to end any cycle of wounds?

☐ 4. In 2 Samuel 5, we hear how all twelve tribes of Israel unite under David and make a covenant with him to be their king. How does this covenantal relationship reflect David's unique role in God's plan for Israel?

☐ 5. David desires to bring the Ark of the Covenant to Jerusalem. Once it is safely there, he experiences "rest from all his enemies around him." With his ability to rest, David turns to improving his and his people's proper worship of God. What does this teach us about the connection between true rest and true worship? How can we rest better so that we may worship better this week?

....

Weekly Challenge

How can you bring more intention to your prayer time, just as David did for his kingdom? This week, create a designated spot to pray, light a candle at the beginning of your prayer time, or visit the closest Adoration chapel. At the end of the week, reflect on how bringing intentionality to your prayer time affected you.

Group Activity

When God granted peace and David was able to rest from his enemies, David focused on reforming the nation's way of worship. He desired to improve and purify their service to God. With the group, discuss the importance of true Sabbath rest. What does this look like for you? What constitutes true and right rest and leisure? What does not? How can we improve in this? What difference would it make in your worship and your week?

Note of Hope

Before all his battles, David reaches out to the Lord in prayer for instruction. God will guide us, too. He gives us the gifts of the Holy Spirit: wisdom, understanding, counsel, fortitude, knowledge, piety, and fear of the Lord. This week, let us ask the Lord for an increase in the gifts of the Holy Spirit.

SCRIPTURE VERSE TO REMEMBER

"Therefore you are great, O Lord God; for there is none like you, and there is no God besides you, according to all that we have heard with our ears."

2 SAMUEL 7:22

Prayer Intentions

Response (R): There is none like you, God.

May all nations unite in their praise of you: **R.**

Help us seek true rest so that we may practice true worship: **R.**

May we spend each Sabbath in praise of you: **R.**

You call each of us by name: **R.**

May we establish you as King of our families and our hearts: **R.**

In this year spent with your Word: **R.**

Catechism Connection

These paragraphs in the *Catechism* may be helpful for reflection on the Scripture read this week in *The Bible in a Year*: CCC 1698, 1788, 1817, 2235

Highlight from the *Catechism*:

- "Hope is the theological virtue by which we desire the kingdom of heaven and eternal life as our happiness, placing our trust in Christ's promises and relying not on our own strength, but on the help of the grace of the Holy Spirit" (CCC 1817).

Closing Prayer

Father in heaven, we give you thanks and praise. You are a good God, you are a good Father, and you continue to meet us. You forgive us completely, but you also call us to complete repentance. You offer forgiveness totally, but you also call us to totally come back to you. And so help us, please, Father. Help us do that. Help us to come back totally so that your mercy may totally transform us, your grace may totally transform us, and your love may totally renew us. Lord God, bring us back to you. Let your face shine on us, and we shall be saved. In Jesus' name we pray. Amen.

Opening Prayer

Father in heaven, we thank you for this season of our lives. We thank you for guiding us and speaking to us, for shaping our eyes, our hearts, and our minds by your Word. We ask you to please fill us with a spirit of courage and purpose. Fill us with the wisdom to be able to know which actions to take and to know which actions to refrain from taking. In Jesus' name, we pray. Amen.

Reflection with Scripture

☐ 1. David seeks out Mephibosheth, the son of Jonathan, in order to show him kindness. Fr. Mike encourages us to ask ourselves, "Is there anyone around me right now that I can show kindness to for the Lord's sake?" What is our response to this?

☐ 2. David commits adultery with Uriah's wife, Bathsheba. He then deepens his sin by ordering Uriah, one of his thirty-seven mighty men, to be killed in battle. Are there any sins that may have started small but are growing in my heart because I have left them unchecked?

☐ 3. Nathan the prophet speaks wisdom and truth to David, confronting him about his sin. Nathan's boldness of heart teaches us the importance of having someone we are accountable to in our spiritual journey. How can we receive constructive criticism from others with humility? How can we offer respectful and loving correction to others when needed?

☐ 4. Like David's story shows, often our sins are due to neglecting our daily duty and not doing the task that the Lord has set in front of us to do. Instead of going to battle as he should, David sends Joab and other Israelites to fight. Likewise, he does not take the action he should to discipline his son Amnon. How can I guard against giving in to complacency and sloth each day? Do I need to re-order my daily routine in any way to fulfill the duties of my vocation and state of life?

☐ 5. First Chronicles focuses on the Royal Kingdom and Temple worship. The king's role is deeply connected with proper worship of God. Do we pray for our Church, nation, and world leaders each day? How can we better incorporate this intention into our daily prayer?

Weekly Challenge

This week, choose a few songs of praise or classical liturgical music pieces to listen to. What are your favorite songs of worship? Are there specific lyrics that touch your heart? How can you cultivate a heart of praise in each moment?

Group Activity

Host an evening of praise at a group member's home or at your parish. You can ask group members who know how to play an instrument to lead, or have recorded praise music to listen to. Before the praise begins, ask people to voice their prayer petitions.

Note of Hope

Our daily tasks and duties, our vocation and work, are a path to holiness. Instead of distracting ourselves and others, may we build up others in their vocational duties and, in so doing, live out our vocations fully. Whenever we are tempted to give in to complacency, let us remember that God gives us grace upon grace to accomplish each moment's task. At the end of each day, let us humbly entrust all our works, joys, failings, trials, and triumphs to God's abundant mercy.

SCRIPTURE VERSE TO REMEMBER

"I acknowledged my sin to you, and I did not hide my iniquity;
I said, 'I will confess my transgressions to the LORD';
then you forgave the guilt of my sin."
PSALM 32:5

Prayer Intentions

Response (R): Lord, we praise you!
When others show us mercy and kindness: *R.*
When you move our hearts to do works of love: *R.*
When others hold us accountable for our sinful actions: *R.*
In our daily tasks and duties: *R.*
In the grace of the present moment: *R.*
As we place our trust in you for our future: *R.*
In this year spent with your Word: *R.*

Catechism Connection

These paragraphs in the *Catechism* may be helpful for reflection on the Scripture read this week in *The Bible in a Year*: CCC 1455, 1469, 1899, 2447

Highlight from the *Catechism*:
- "The works of mercy are charitable actions by which we come to the aid of our neighbor in his spiritual and bodily necessities" (CCC 2447).

Closing Prayer

Father in heaven, we praise you, and we give you thanks. Lord, we offer this word of trust and confidence in you and your goodness and faithfulness. Even in times of insecurity, even in times of uncertainty, even in times of great trial and battle where the enemy is winning, we declare our trust in you, this day and every day. In Jesus' name, we pray. Amen.

Opening Prayer

Father in heaven, as we follow the story of David, we ask that you please help us to discern in our own hearts where we need to be convicted of sin. Of all the voices that we hear in the course of the day, let yours be the one that is the loudest, that is the clearest, and that goes directly to our hearts. In Jesus' name, we pray. Amen.

Reflection with Scripture

☐ 1. When David takes a census of the people in 1 Chronicles 21, he is doing something evil in the sight of the Lord because he is trying to establish himself over the people instead of establishing God over the people. David repents of this decision, yet there is a consequence to his actions. How can we maintain a heart of gratitude for God's forgiveness while we experience the natural consequences of our sins?

☐ 2. Even though it is David's son Solomon who will build the Temple, we hear in 1 Chronicles 22 that David makes preparations for the Temple by choosing a site and gathering materials for it to be built. How can we better prepare for the future, both spiritually and materially, so that those who come after us are properly equipped to live out their duties?

☐ 3. David sets an example for us: he deeply sins, yet he acknowledges the gravity of his sin and seeks forgiveness. How can we imitate David's humility in acknowledging the truth about our actions and repenting of our sins?

☐ 4. In reflecting on Absalom and David, Fr. Mike poses a question that each of us should ask of ourselves: "How often have others suffered because of my sins?" Do I take accountability and full ownership of my actions? Is there someone today who is affected by my sins? If so, how can I take steps to make this right?

☐ 5. In 1 Chronicles 26, we are introduced to the gatekeepers of the Temple. Often, we disregard certain jobs or roles in our society as menial when, in fact, they are sanctifying. Two things that make saints stand out are that they saw their work as a path to holiness and that they loved people no matter their status. How can we better imitate the saints in these two areas?

Weekly Challenge

Find a piece of sacred art depicting God the Father. Set aside some time to meditate on the mercy of God, who claims you as his beloved son or daughter in Baptism. How has listening to the *Bible in a Year* podcast helped you better understand God's love for his people in both the Old and New Testaments?

Group Activity

As a group, listen to or read the lyrics to the song that Fr. Mike references in day 136, "When David Heard" by Eric Whitacre. Invite group members to share which parts of the song they find moving.

Note of Hope

God has claimed us as his sons and daughters. May we always rejoice in our baptismal grace and, in turn, claim God as our good and gentle Father. We are not just his creatures; we are willed and loved into being. We are his own. We have reason to rejoice in thanksgiving that he has called each of us by name. We are loved by our Creator.

SCRIPTURE VERSE TO REMEMBER

"The LORD lives; and blessed be my rock,
and exalted be my God, the rock of my salvation."
2 SAMUEL 22:47

Prayer Intentions

Response (R): The Lord is our rock, our fortress, and our deliverer.
As we claim you as our good and gentle Father, let us pray: *R.*
In times of mourning, let us pray: *R.*
In reflecting on our past, let us pray: *R.*
When we realize the gravity of our sin, let us pray: *R.*
When we seek your forgiveness, let us pray: *R.*
In this year spent with your Word, let us pray: *R.*

Catechism Connection

These paragraphs in the *Catechism* may be helpful for reflection on the Scripture

read this week in *The Bible in a Year*: CCC 1140, 1810, 2713, 2097

Highlight from the *Catechism*:

- "To adore God is to acknowledge him as God, as the Creator and Savior, the Lord and Master of everything that exists" (CCC 2097).

Closing Prayer

Father in heaven, we give you praise and glory, and we bless your name. We praise your name and holiness. All glory is yours. All praise and thanksgiving belong to you for who you are and for what you've done in our lives. And so, Lord, preserve us from resentment, preserve us from corruption, and preserve us from despair and discouragement. Help us to be filled with your courage and your grace, and therefore to be able to let our lives be signs of praise and thanksgiving. In Jesus' name, we pray. Amen.

Opening Prayer

Father in heaven, we give you praise in all things, and God, thank you so much for Psalm 42. We so often get assaulted by that question, "Where is your God? If you believe in him, and if he is there for you and loves you, then point him out to me. Where is he?" Lord God, in those moments, we might be our own accuser, the Evil One might be the accuser, or those around us might be the accuser who asked that question. Yet, in this moment, Lord, we know where you are. You are with us. You are for us. And you are beside us at all times. Lord God, we give you praise, and we thank you. We make that declaration of faith even when it is hard for us to know where you are or sense your presence. We have faith. We have faith that you are faithful to your promises. And you have said you will be with us forever. You are with us at all times. Without you, we can do nothing. And so with you, we can do all things. Father, keep us close to you and never let us be parted from you. In Jesus' name, we pray. Amen.

Reflection with Scripture

☐ 1. During the last days of David, we hear about his mighty men. David was able to do all he did as king because of their assistance, especially in battles. Do we acknowledge those around us who have helped us come to the place where we are now? Who helps you fight your daily battles? How can you better acknowledge that person's unique gifts and say thank you?

☐ 2. In 1 Chronicles 28:9, we hear how David instructs Solomon to serve God. Do we actively seek God out each day? When are some moments that we can seek him?

☐ 3. David gives all the materials to build the Temple freely and wholeheartedly. Do I hold back and give halfheartedly to God and to others in my worship? In my service? In my gifts? In my tithing? Do I fear the lack instead of trusting in his abundance?

☐ 4. One of the main narratives in the books of Kings is the rise and fall of the Davidic Kingdom. At the start of 1 Kings, we see that David, who rules the kingdom, does not know what is going on within his own family. How can we avoid falling into a similar trap of focusing on our secondary roles at the cost of our primary vocation? How can we prioritize our duties each day?

☐ 5. David's spoken advice to Solomon did not always align with David's lived-out example. Do I practice what I preach? If not, what holds me back? How can I grow in integrity?

Weekly Challenge

Take time this week to discern if there are any activities, ministries, or people that are distracting you from the duties of your primary vocation. Honestly ask yourself if you are stewarding your time wisely. Is there anything that you need to say no to in order to better focus on what God is calling you to do? Ask the Holy Spirit to give you clarity in this.

Group Activity

Pray the Divine Mercy Chaplet as a group. Invite members to take turns leading each decade. As you pray, reflect on David's acknowledgment of God's mercy. Offer any petitions you have as a group before you pray.

Note of Hope

God has gifted us his Mother and his saints to intercede on our behalf. He has sent his only Son, Jesus, the greatest Intercessor, to save us from our sins. We have a host in heaven championing us to join them in Beatitude. Yet the Kingdom of God begins here, right now. Let us realize that we are part of his Communion of Saints and that he will continue to give us all the graces we need to fight the good fight of faith.

SCRIPTURE VERSE TO REMEMBER

"Then David said to Solomon his son, 'Be strong and of good courage, and do it. Fear not, be not dismayed; for the LORD God, even my God, is with you. He will not fail you or forsake you, until all the work for the service of the house of the LORD is finished.'"
1 CHRONICLES 28:20

Prayer Intentions

Response (R): Give us an understanding mind that we may discern between good and evil, O God!

In our leadership roles: **R.**

In our vocations: **R.**

In all the decisions we make: **R.**

As we discern the right path: **R.**

When we plan our days: **R.**

When we pray: **R.**

In this year spent with your Word: **R.**

Catechism Connection

These paragraphs in the *Catechism* may be helpful for reflection on the Scripture read this week in *The Bible in a Year*: CCC 1831, 2059, 2099, 2223

Highlight from the *Catechism*:

- "The gift of the Commandments is the gift of God himself and his holy will. In making his will known, God reveals himself to his people" (CCC 2059).

Closing Prayer

Father in heaven, we give you praise. You do hear our prayers. Every time we talk to you, Lord, you hear our voices. You know the longing of our hearts. You know the depth of our prayer. You also know our distraction. You know how easily we can be distracted from loving you with our whole heart, with our whole mind, with our whole strength. You know how easily it is that we are turned aside from you. And so, we thank you for being able to hear through all the noise, cutting through all of the distraction, cutting through all of the turmoil that our hearts can experience because you know our hearts. You not only know the peace in our hearts, but you also know the trouble in our hearts. And so, we ask you, please once again, let your ears be open. Let your eyes be open to see who we are, to see us truly, and to hear our voice, and to hear our prayers this day and every day. We make this prayer in Jesus' name. Amen.

Opening Prayer

Father in heaven, we thank you and give you praise. We thank you so much for the gift of your Word. We thank you for the gift of peace and deliverance, Lord God, because you deliver us from our enemies. Now, even when we're in distress, even when it seems like the world is crashing around us, even when it seems like there are obstacles—and truly, there are obstacles in our lives—you make us lie down and sleep. Lord God, when we can't sleep, when we cannot find rest, when our minds are so busy and scattered and we feel so stretched, so thin, then we can realize that we need to rely upon your grace and your mercy. We acknowledge our weakness so we can accept your power. And we know your grace is sufficient for every one of our days, for every one of our moments. And so we give you praise. In Jesus' name, we pray. Amen.

Reflection with Scripture

☐ 1. The Temple was built in such a way that no noise was made at the site (see 1 Kings 6:7). Fr. Mike talks about the importance of silence in God's house. Let's look again at paragraph 66 of Benedict XVI's apostolic exhortation *Verbum Domini,* where he details this holy silence: "The great patristic tradition teaches us that the mysteries of Christ all involve silence. Only in silence can the word of God find a home in us." Do we take enough time to be silent? How can we improve in this area?

☐ 2. In 2 Chronicles 9, we hear about Solomon's wealth increasing, so much so that even his shields were made of beaten gold. Fr. Mike points out that golden shields would be too soft and heavy for battle; they were just for show. He poses the question, "Is Solomon becoming the image of strength while no longer being actually strong?" Are there areas of my life where I desire to appear better than I am in compensation for a lack of virtue?

☐ 3. As the Ark of the Covenant was brought into the Temple, God's presence came into the Temple in an overwhelming and powerful way (see 1 Kings 8:11). Is there a time you experienced the Lord's presence in a powerful way?

☐ 4. In Ecclesiastes 3:1, we hear that "for everything there is a season." How would you describe the season of life you are in?

☐ 5. In Ecclesiastes 5:7, we hear about dreaming. Sometimes we can talk a lot about our dreams, but not work toward fulfilling them. What is one dream that you desire to fulfill? What is one action that you could take today to work toward your dream?

Weekly Challenge

As the Queen of Sheba visits Solomon, we see his external wealth and the glory of his kingship. However, shortly afterward, we hear Solomon's demise begin to take place as he breaks the three Mosaic Laws that were established to limit the power of kings (see Deuteronomy 17:16–17). Solomon falls into the three-fold temptation that St. John warns about in 1 John 2:16—"the lust of the flesh and the lust of the eyes and the pride of life." Solomon chooses many wives (lust of the flesh), gold (lust of the eyes), and horses and weaponry (pride of life). This week, read the story of Jesus' temptation in the desert in Matthew chapter 4 and reflect on how Jesus overcame these three temptations. Spend time in prayer asking God to deliver you from any temptation of these three sins.

Group Activity

Find an image of Solomon's Temple. Discuss with the group if this is what you pictured when you heard the description, or if you were picturing something else. Share anything that strikes you, specifically with the layout of the Temple.

Note of Hope

Christ desires our true freedom. Through his example, grace, and triumph against evil, he equips us to break the chains of sin. As we are tempted in this life, let us remember that he is with us, he was tempted too, and he gives us the power through his Spirit to overcome each temptation. When we fail, we know that we can run to him in humility, trusting that he is always waiting for us to return to him. What a joy to have him as our Savior!

SCRIPTURE VERSE TO REMEMBER

"Two are better than one, because they have a good reward for their toil."
ECCLESIASTES 4:9

Prayer Intentions

Response (R): With you, there is a time and season for all things.
In our hopeful wait, help us remember: *R.*
During days that we struggle, help us remember: *R.*
When we are unable to do all that we desire, help us remember: *R.*
As we help others carry their crosses, help us remember: *R.*
As we discern your will, help us remember: *R.*
In this year spent with your Word, help us remember: *R.*

St. Rita of Cascia, pray for us and all in need, especially for impossible causes and for women who have suffered abuse.
Feast Day: May 22

Catechism Connection

These paragraphs in the *Catechism* may be helpful for reflection on the Scripture read this week in *The Bible in a Year*: CCC 1723, 2098, 2113

Highlight from the *Catechism*:

- "Idolatry is not just worshiping false gods. It remains a constant temptation to displace God with anything else—power, pleasure, or possessions" (CCC 2113).

Closing Prayer

Father in heaven, we give you praise and glory. Thank you so much for revealing your Son to us. You so loved the world that you gave your only Son that all who believe in him might not perish but might have eternal life. And so we thank you, and we give you praise. Thank you so much for giving us the good news and the opportunity to hear this good news. So please receive our praise. Help us to be converted. Call us to be your disciples, to follow after you with all our heart, mind, soul, and strength, and to love you with everything we are and everything we have. In Jesus' name, we pray. Amen.

Opening Prayer

Father in heaven, we honor and love you for the gift of your Son, Jesus, and for the gift of knowing his teaching and heart. He is the Word of the Father. When we see him, we see you. Thank you for these moments and the images of Jesus in Mark's Gospel. In Jesus' name, we pray. Amen.

Reflection with Scripture

☐ 1. St. Mark's Gospel uses the word "immediately" often, pointing to the urgency Jesus had in proclaiming the Good News. Do we share in his persistence? What strikes us the most when we hear the word "immediately" used so often throughout this Gospel? What may God be trying to tell us through this word?

☐ 2. Jesus heals and restores people throughout the Gospel of Mark. What ways does the Church follow in his footsteps by helping people carry the cross of physical suffering while also healing the soul through the Sacraments?

☐ 3. In Mark 2, a paralytic is brought to Jesus through the roof by four men. Am I persistent in prayer for my friends? Do I go to great lengths to help them be spiritually well and whole? Who is one person in my life that I could pray persistently for?

☐ 4. After ministering to others, the apostles return to Jesus, and he highlights to them the importance of rest. Do we realize that Jesus does not want us to burn out in our work, vocation, and ministry, but rather desires to rest with us so that we may be renewed in him? Is there someone we know who needs rest and renewal? How can we help give them the space, ability, and encouragement to rest? What sacrifices might we need to offer to help make their true rest possible?

☐ 5. In Mark 15, we hear how the battalion of soldiers was called together to mock Jesus during his Passion. Have I ever mocked someone? Is there someone who comes to mind that I need to apologize to as a result? Have I ever been mocked? Is there someone who comes to mind that I need to forgive?

Weekly Challenge

When Jesus saw the poor widow offer her two coins, he praised her for her generous gift (see Mark 12:42–44). Take some time this week to reflect on how you can give God your "whole living." What virtues, like generosity and temperance, can you pray for and practice that help you steward your life as a gift? What sacrifices are you called to make in your life? What are some ways that God may be asking you to simplify?

Group Activity

As a group, share different ministries that are important to you and why. Together, pick one to donate to this week. No contribution is too small. As a group, pray for the ministries that were shared, and write a note to the ministry that you decided to donate to.

Note of Hope

Often, we feel like we have nothing left to give. Remember, the Lord calls us to "come away" with him and "rest awhile." We have the incredible opportunity to "come and see" Jesus in the Sacraments, especially in the Eucharist. Rest with him there. Lay your burdens before your King, who is so eager to help you. Adore your Creator. Listen to what he has to tell you. And after receiving him and becoming a living tabernacle for him, those who encounter you can encounter him through you.

SCRIPTURE VERSE TO REMEMBER

"And he said to them, 'Go into all the world and preach the gospel to the whole creation.'"
MARK 16:15

Prayer Intentions

Response (R): Let us share how much the Lord has done for us!
As we proclaim your Gospel to all the ends of the earth: *R.*
When we give our whole living to you: *R.*
As we persistently pray for our friends: *R.*
When you calm the storms of our life: *R.*
Because we need a greater humility of heart, to be servants rather than be served: *R.*
As we seek true rest and renewal with you: *R.*
In this year spent with your Word: *R.*

Catechism Connection

These paragraphs in the *Catechism* may be helpful for reflection on the Scripture read this week in *The Bible in a Year*: CCC 394, 754, 2816

Highlight from the *Catechism*:
*   "Christ is the head and the shepherd who leads us to eternal life" (CCC 754).

Closing Prayer

Father in heaven, thank you for giving us hope, because in the face of our own death, suffering, pain, and sin, we have no hope if we are on our own. But Lord God, you have sent your Son to bear our sin, to transform our suffering, and to conquer the power of death and transform it so it is no longer the enemy. Death gives birth to us in your presence. She brings us from this world into the next. She brings us from this life into eternal life with you. And that is only possible because of your love, Father, because of the love of your Son, Jesus Christ, and what he did for us. Father, please send your Holy Spirit upon us right now and transform in our hearts what needs to be transformed, bring to life what is dead, and heal what is broken. Please Lord God, forgive what needs forgiveness. In Jesus' name, we pray. Amen.

Reflection with Scripture

☐ 1. After the death of his father, Solomon, King Rehoboam took counsel with both the older men and the younger men. Referencing this, Fr. Mike asks us to consider where we look for counsel. Do we seek out those who are sources of wisdom, or do we look to the people who agree with us?

☐ 2. Out of fear, Jeroboam, the leader in the Northern Kingdom, makes two golden calves and encourages his people to practice the sin of idolatry. Often, the idols in our lives can grow subtly in our hearts. How can we resist the temptation to make an idol out of any political entity or leader?

☐ 3. Fr. Mike says, "We can know we give the Lord our hearts by our actions." Like Asa in 2 Chronicles 15, how can we seek God with all our hearts through our actions?

☐ 4. In the second chapter of Song of Solomon, we hear the bride say, "My beloved is mine and I am his" (Song of Solomon 2:16). Do I see Jesus as my beloved? My greatest love? Do I love him with this intimacy of heart?

☐ 5. Elijah challenges the people of Israel to make a decision for the Lord, but they are silent (see 1 Kings 18:21). Am I lukewarm in my faith right now? Do I give just a portion of my heart to the Lord, and another portion to the things of this world? How would my life change if I decided to wholeheartedly follow the Lord?

Weekly Challenge

The widow of Zarephath had every reason to turn Elijah away: she was a widow in famine with a son to care for. Yet she risked it all in generosity and trust. This week, reflect on whether you are holding tightly to a part of your life out of fear. In what area do you need to "risk it all" by trusting the Lord and his providence through your generous offering?

Group Activity

The widow of Zarephath is a beautiful example of hospitality. She could have focused on her lack, but she decided to trust in God's abundance. St. Thomas Aquinas wrote a homily entitled "The Law of Hospitality," in which he shares that we are biblically exhorted to practice great hospitality and gives four reasons to do so.[5] As a group, discuss whether hospitality is something you enjoy or struggle with. Brainstorm ways to show hospitality to others. What can the widow of Zarephath teach us about hospitality?

---

5. See Aquinas, "Homily III, The Law of Hospitality," in *Ninety-Nine Homilies of Saint Thomas Aquinas: Upon the Epistles and Gospels for Forty-Nine Sundays of the Christian Year Homily III, The Law of Hospitality* (London: Aeterna Press, 2015).

Note of Hope

God has chosen you to live in this time in history. Through your baptism and with the help of the Church, you have been equipped with his grace to triumph over sin and death. You are his light in this world. You are called to live a life of sanctity and generous love. Do not fear the lack, but trust in his abundant plan for your life.

SCRIPTURE VERSE TO REMEMBER

"His speech is most sweet, and he is altogether desirable. This is my beloved and this is my friend, O daughters of Jerusalem."
SONG OF SOLOMON 5:16

Prayer Intentions

Response (R): We will exult and rejoice in you, O Lord!
As we invite people into our homes: *R.*
When we practice hospitality: *R.*
As you open our minds and hearts to the promptings of the Holy Spirit: *R.*
As we strive to see you in all we meet: *R.*
So that we may be cheerful givers: *R.*
So that we may wholeheartedly choose you: *R.*
In this year spent with your Word: *R.*

St. Justin Martyr, pray for us all, especially philosophers, apologists, and those defending the Faith.
Feast Day: June 1

Catechism Connection

These paragraphs in the *Catechism* may be helpful for reflection on the Scripture read this week in *The Bible in a Year*: CCC 682, 2119, 2656, 2709

Highlight from the *Catechism*:

- "When he comes at the end of time to judge the living and the dead, the glorious Christ will reveal the secret disposition of hearts and will render to each man according to his works and according to his acceptance or refusal of grace" (CCC 682).

Closing Prayer

Father in heaven, we are the object of your love. You are eternal, mysterious, all good—and yet you love us. You pursue us and desire us, even in our brokenness. You still choose us. Help us to give you permission to be chosen by you and to choose you back. Help us receive your love and love you in return. In Jesus' name, we pray. Amen.

Opening Prayer

Father, we know that love is as strong as death. It led you to die for us, to draw us near, to make us your children, and to love us as you desire. Set me as a seal upon your heart, as a seal upon your arm. Help us live every day as yours, as your beloved. In Jesus' name, we pray. Amen.

Reflection with Scripture

☐ 1. One of the missions of Elijah is to call Israel out of its idolatrous worship. When is a time that you displayed bold courage in leading people to God instead of worldly idols?

☐ 2. We hear about how Amaziah, who followed the Lord, turned away from him and began worshiping the idols of the people he had just defeated. Fr. Mike invites us to inspect our own hearts and ask God, "Lord, I am faithful on the outside, but deep inside, am I hollow?" Is my love of God firmly rooted and unwavering?

☐ 3. In 2 Kings 3, we read how Jehoram became king over Israel and "clung to the sin of Jeroboam." What are the ways that we can break our attachments to sin? What Sacraments in our Church aid us in this?

☐ 4. The Lord blessed the Shunammite couple for their hospitality and generosity to the prophet Elisha. Throughout it all, their trust and hope in the Lord were stretched to grow. In what ways have you experienced blessings because of hospitality and generosity?

☐ 5. Like Naaman, our success in life means very little without God. We can have reputation and honor, yet without God, we lack what truly matters. In what areas of life am I successful? How can I offer that success to the Lord and thank him for it?

Weekly Challenge

Take time to reflect this week on something or someone that may be causing you heartache right now. Like the Shunammite couple, how can you turn to the Lord with your pain during this time? God does not want to play with your heart. He desires to bless you; he desires your faithfulness and holiness. How can this suffering be a path to holiness?

Group Activity

Spend time in prayer reflecting on the fruits of the Holy Spirit: charity (love), joy, peace, patience, kindness, goodness, generosity, gentleness, faithfulness, modesty, self-control, and chastity. Discuss with the group which of these stands out to you the most. Which is the fruit that God is calling you to grow in? Pray out loud with each group member for a double portion of this fruit.

Note of Hope

You have a role in the Church. Your life has meaning and value. You are a thought of God, who fashioned you and loved you into being. You are irreplaceable. Knowing that you have a mission and what that mission is forms your own heart and the hearts of those you will minister to. You and others will be grounded in his love. Do not be afraid to live out your mission. He is with you.

SCRIPTURE VERSE TO REMEMBER

*"For I desire mercy and not sacrifice,
the knowledge of God, rather than burnt offerings."*
HOSEA 6:6

Prayer Intentions

Response (R): Lord, help make us holy.
We pray for all those struggling in our parish community: **R.**
We pray that we may always embrace your words of life: **R.**
We pray for the grace to be patient and forgiving this week: **R.**
We pray for all those who have strayed from the Faith: **R.**
We pray for grace to break our grasp from worldly idols: **R.**
We pray for help to frequent your Sacraments: **R.**
In this year spent with your Word: **R.**

St. Anthony of Padua, pray for us and all in need, especially the poor, travelers, and those who have lost items.
Feast Day: June 13

Catechism Connection

These paragraphs in the *Catechism* may be helpful for reflection on the Scripture read this week in *The Bible in a Year:* CCC 1503, 2055, 2603

Highlight from the *Catechism*:

- "When someone asks him, 'Which commandment in the Law is the greatest?' Jesus replies: 'You shall love the Lord your God with all your heart, and with all your soul, and with all your mind. This is the greatest and first commandment. And a second is like it: You shall love your neighbor as yourself'" (CCC 2055).

Closing Prayer

Father in heaven, we give you praise and thanks, for your mercy is toward those who fear you. As far as the east is from the west, so far do you remove our transgressions. Your mercy is limitless, given most when we need it most and deserve it least. You know our weakness and still give us grace. Help us to say yes to you this day and every day. In Jesus' name, we pray. Amen.

Reflection with Scripture

☐ 1. Elisha not only saved the life of his friend, the Shunammite woman, in the famine, but he also helped restore her land after the famine. Where do we turn when we are in a spiritual drought, a spiritual "famine"? What friends or family help restore our spirits?

☐ 2. One of the powerful realities of free will is that we must choose. The prophets remind us of this truth. Are my daily choices turning me closer to God or away from him?

☐ 3. In David's Psalms we hear his honest prayers. He offers his real and raw heart to God in prayer. Why might this be challenging to do in prayer? How can we open ourselves more fully to God when we pray?

☐ 4. Amos warns the people of Israel about a life of complacency. The root word of complacency is from the Latin *complacere*, meaning, "to please." Do I live in a way that prioritizes my own pleasure? How can I grow in a life pleasing to God?

☐ 5. When he initially hears God's command, the prophet Jonah flees in fear. How can fear hold us back from doing God's will? In what ways do we flee from doing what God is asking of us?

Weekly Challenge
Do an act of love for someone who helped you when you experienced spiritual dryness. This action could be praying for that person, writing a thank you note, or sending a small gift. Or, do an act of love for someone you know who is going through a spiritual drought. For example, invite that person to pray with you, go for a walk together, or share an outing for coffee.

Group Activity
As a group, make "blessing bags" to keep in the car to give to any homeless person you might pass by. First make a list of items: toothbrush, toothpaste, deodorant, socks, gift cards, wipes, etc., and invite each group member to sign up to provide one kind of item. Then fill the bags together. Include a handwritten note or Bible verse in each bag.

Note of Hope

In our spiritual poverty, the Lord came to give us the wealth of his grace and gifts. He desires to lavish us with his goodness. In our sorrows, in our dryness, and in our inconsistencies, he shows us true joy and steadfastness. Just as he washed the feet of his disciples, he shows us that true meaning and joy flow from a heart of generosity and humility. May we always choose a life in him.

SCRIPTURE VERSE TO REMEMBER

"The Lord will fulfil his purpose for me; your mercy, O Lord, endures for ever. Do not forsake the work of your hands."
PSALM 138:8

Prayer Intentions

Response (R): You are a gracious God, abounding in mercy.
We pray for an end to all injustice and abuse inflicted on the poor: *R.*
We pray that we may steward our finances for the building up of your kingdom here on earth: *R.*
We pray in thanksgiving for the gift of our free will, and that we may always choose you: *R.*
We pray for the people who have restored us in times of spiritual famine: *R.*
As we seek to live a life pleasing to you, we pray: *R.*
In this year spent in your Word, we pray: *R.*

Catechism Connection

These paragraphs in the *Catechism* may be helpful for reflection on the Scripture read this week in *The Bible in a Year*: CCC 713, 1694, 2567, 1423

Highlight from the *Catechism*:

- "In prayer, the faithful God's initiative of love always comes first; our own first step is always a response. As God gradually reveals himself and reveals man to himself, prayer appears as a reciprocal call, a covenant drama. Through words and actions, this drama engages the heart. It unfolds throughout the whole history of salvation" (CCC 2567).

Closing Prayer

Father in heaven, we give you praise. You formed us and have known us through and through. We can never escape you—nor would we want to. Help us let you find us, to seek you and not run. Help us to stop, turn back, and be found by you, the God who loves us. Help us to let ourselves be loved in this unstoppable, inescapable way. In Jesus' name, we pray. Amen.

Opening Prayer

Father in heaven, thank you for your Word and your love. Thank you for calling us back to you. We face not just human foes but the true enemies—the world, flesh, and the Devil. Protect us from these snares. Help us be vigilant and wise, with eyes open to the traps before us. Give us courage to call out to you and to fight, never trading truth for comfort. Help us be yours in all things. In Jesus' name, we pray. Amen.

Reflection with Scripture

☐ 1. What lessons does the Assyrian Exile teach us that we can apply to our Church today?

☐ 2. In Psalm 145:8, we hear a description of the Lord. If someone asked you to describe God, how would you respond?

☐ 3. In the midst of great opposition and danger, Hezekiah purifies Temple worship and removes false worship, all while relying upon the Lord. What are your biggest spiritual takeaways from Hezekiah's example of courage and trust?

☐ 4. Hezekiah pleaded with the Lord for extra time in life, and the Lord granted him fifteen more years to live. Yet Hezekiah did not use that time to grow in holiness. Do you see each new day as an opportunity to grow in holiness? Do you see areas of your life that are stagnant? How can you reawaken your soul, through the gifts the Church offers, to seek holiness each day?

☐   5. Josiah became king at a very young age and led one of the greatest reforms of Judah. How can we better support our youth in their journey to God and with God?

Weekly Challenge

Take time this week to contemplate Micah 6:8. Make three columns on a piece of paper: Justice, Kindness, Humility. Underneath each section, write down some ideas about how you can grow in each of these three areas.

Group Activity

As a group, pray for young people. Ask group members to write the first names of several young people they have in mind on index cards and place the names in a basket. Then, pray the Rosary together for the intentions of those young people and all the youth of the parish.

Note of Hope

With God, all things are possible. It is through his love and grace that we are able to do justice, love kindness, and walk humbly with him. Through his Bride, the Church, he gifts us the Sacraments to strengthen us to live out these three requirements. He has also generously gifted us the Communion of Saints, of which we are a part. May we always call on God and the saints' intercession as we strive to grow in holiness each day.

SCRIPTURE VERSE TO REMEMBER

"He has showed you, O man, what is good; and what does the LORD require of you but to do justice, and to love kindness, and to walk humbly with your God?"
MICAH 6:8

Prayer Intentions

Response (R): Generous and good Father, hear our prayer.
For the protection and the purity of the world's youth: **R.**
That we may use the time you give us to grow in holiness: **R.**
That we may give good spiritual gifts to future generations: **R.**
That we may always do justice, love kindness, and walk humbly before you: **R.**
In this year spent with your Word: **R.**

Saints Peter and Paul, pray for us all and especially for the Universal Church, Rome, and fishermen.
Feast Day: June 29

Catechism **Connection**

These paragraphs in the *Catechism* may be helpful for reflection on the Scripture read this week in *The Bible in a Year*: CCC 1428, 2114, 2737, 2787

Highlight from the *Catechism*:

· "Christ's call to conversion continues to resound in the lives of Christians ... This endeavor of conversion is not just a human work. It is the movement of a 'contrite heart,' drawn and moved by grace to respond to the merciful love of God who loved us" (CCC 1428).

Closing Prayer

Father, thank you for your gift and for revealing your heart and wisdom to us. As we journey through Proverbs, increase our wisdom and our ability to see and understand what is right and true. Help us truly listen, not just know, so we may wisely follow you and wisely lead those entrusted to us—our families, friends, and others in our world. In Jesus' name, we pray. Amen.

Opening Prayer

Father in heaven, we thank you and give you praise. Thank you for your wisdom, which created the world. When we listen and keep your ways, we are happy and blessed. Help us hear instruction and be wise. Help us watch daily at the gates of wisdom and find wisdom, life, and favor from you. Thank you for this day. We pray all in Jesus' name. Amen.

Reflection with Scripture

☐ 1. Reflecting on Proverbs 10:7, think of someone who has left you a memory of blessing through their life of righteousness.

☐ 2. What are some ways we can discern and hear God's voice when he is calling us to repentance?

☐ 3. The last verses of 2 Chronicles are ones of hope during the time of exile. How does this hope of a promise for restoration reveal God's continuous mercy and care for his people?

☐ 4. Tobit describes himself as having "walked in the ways of truth and righteousness all the days" of his life and "performed many acts of charity" to his countrymen and brethren (see Tobit 1:3). Could I describe myself the same way? How can I grow in charity?

☐ 5. Both Tobit's prayer and Sarah's prayer were "heard in the presence of the glory of the Great God" (Tobit 3:16) at the same moment. What does this teach us about the power of vocalizing our heart's needs to God through prayer?

Weekly Challenge

This week, reflect on the angel Raphael's name and the meaning behind it. If you don't already know it, look up the meaning of your name and ponder the ways that you exemplify its meaning. Read paragraphs 2156–2159 in the *Catechism* that teach about the Christian name. Write down, or highlight in your heart, anything that stands out to you in this section.

Group Activity

Isaiah responds to Ahaz's lack of trust with a prophecy (see Isaiah 7:14). Immanuel means, "God is with us." With your group, discuss the ways in which this prophecy was partially fulfilled in Hezekiah and completely fulfilled in Jesus. Share ways in which we can help make the Church a place where people feel the reality of our Immanuel, that God is with us.

Note of Hope

Through the Sacraments, our souls are washed as white as snow. In them, we find Jesus, who makes his home in us. The fruit of the sacramental life is mercy and love. By frequenting the Sacraments, our union with Christ deepens, and we realize nothing on earth fills us like they do. Christ anchors us in reality—and the Sacraments are the greatest reality, the greatest gift and treasure we have on earth.

SCRIPTURE VERSE TO REMEMBER

"For wisdom is better than jewels, and all that you may desire cannot compare with her."
PROVERBS 8:11

Prayer Intentions

Response (R): With joyful hearts, we pray, Lord hear us!

In thanksgiving that you sent your only Son, Immanuel, to save us: **R.**

In gratitude that though our sins are like scarlet, through your Sacraments we are washed white as snow: **R.**

With trust that you care for all those in need of healing: **R.**

For the souls of the righteous who have left us with the memory of their blessing: **R.**

In this year spent with your Word: **R.**

St. Thomas the Apostle, patron saint of architects, builders, and the doubting faithful, pray for us.
Feast Day: July 3

Catechism Connection

These paragraphs in the *Catechism* may be helpful for reflection on the Scripture read this week in *The Bible in a Year*: CCC 50, 336, 1617, 1861, 2559

Highlights from the *Catechism*:

- "Beside each believer stands an angel as protector and shepherd leading him to life" (CCC 336).
- "Prayer is the raising of one's mind and heart to God or the requesting of good things from God" (CCC 2559).

Closing Prayer

Father in heaven, we give you praise and thank you for your Word and wisdom in Proverbs. You call us to choose good and to love you with all our heart, mind, soul, and strength. Hatred stirs strife, but love covers offenses. Help us love you well and wisely in this confusing world. Help us love and be loved well, and to be your image every day. In Jesus' name, we pray. Amen.

Opening Prayer

Father in heaven, we give you praise and glory. Thank you for this opportunity to come back and hear your wisdom, to call us back to you, and remind us of your great consolation. We offer you our thanks. May you be exalted in praise and glory. In Jesus' name, we pray. Amen.

Reflection with Scripture

☐ 1. In Isaiah 11, we hear the prophecy of the coming of Jesus, the descendant of Jesse. Jesse is King David's father and Solomon's grandfather. In what ways is Jesus a "New David" who is even greater than David and Solomon?

☐ 2. The prophets speak to the Israelites as they are suffering in exile, calling them to trust in God. How can suffering bring us closer to God?

☐ 3. In Isaiah 19, we hear that God will bless Egypt and Assyria through an alliance with Israel. Are there people or situations that we are hesitant to believe God will bless? Do we believe that God has the power to convert hearts, even the hearts of our enemies? Do we rejoice in the thought of their conversion? What does this say about the state of our own hearts?

☐ 4. We are called, like the prophets, to be a "watchman" and protect ourselves and those in our care from the dangers of the world (see Isaiah 21:6). In what ways can we improve in this role?

□ 5. In Isaiah 22, we hear that Shebna is the royal steward who tries to place himself in the Davidic royal line. He is replaced by Eliakim. As stewards, these men point to the role of the pope in the Church. Do we pray for the pope's holiness and wisdom? How can we live more deeply as faithful members of the Church?

Weekly Challenge

Is there someone that you dislike that you see is being blessed? How can you thank God for them and their blessings? Take time this week to pray honestly with God about your feelings and ask him for the grace to purify your heart and heal any wounds you may have in relation to this person. Ask him for the grace to rejoice in this person's blessing and ask that he may continue to shower blessings upon the person.

Group Activity

As a group, reflect on St. Michael the Archangel's name and its meaning: "Who is like God." Together, ask his intercession as you pray the Prayer to St. Michael the Archangel:

St. Michael the Archangel, defend us in battle, be our protection against the wickedness and snares of the Devil. May God rebuke him, we humbly pray, and do thou, O Prince of the Heavenly Host, by the power of God, cast into hell Satan and all the evil spirits, who prowl throughout the world seeking the ruin of souls. Amen.

Note of Hope

In Joel 2:12–13, we hear the Lord's call to us to return to him with our entire hearts. "Even now"—even now, with our past or present sins, it is not too late to turn to him. He promises us that he is gracious and merciful, slow to anger, and abounding in mercy. May we take these words of deep love to heart and return to him.

> ### SCRIPTURE VERSE TO REMEMBER
> *"And the Spirit of the LORD shall rest upon him,*
> *the spirit of wisdom and understanding, the spirit of counsel*
> *and might, the spirit of knowledge and the fear of the LORD."*
> ISAIAH 11:2

Prayer Intentions

Response (R): Jesus, we trust in you.

We pray for the grace to be more attentive to our brothers and sisters in need: **R.**

We pray for those discerning their vocation: **R.**

We pray for all the brave "watchmen" who protect the most vulnerable: **R.**

As the day of the Lord draws ever nearer, we pray: **R.**

In this year spent with your Word, we pray: **R.**

St. Augustine Zhao Rong, patron saint of the people of China, pray for us.
Feast Day: July 9

Catechism **Connection**

These paragraphs in the *Catechism* may be helpful for reflection on the Scripture read this week in *The Bible in a Year*: CCC 2091, 1439, 1739

Highlight from the *Catechism*:

- "Man's freedom is limited and fallible. In fact, man failed. He freely sinned. By refusing God's plan of love, he deceived himself and became a slave to sin ... From its inception, human history attests the wretchedness and oppression born of the human heart in consequence of the abuse of freedom" (CCC 1739).

Closing Prayer

Father in heaven, we give you praise and thank you. We want to be counted among the righteous, but often we fail. When we are wicked and not righteous, make us so by your grace. Only you can make us the people we are called to be. We trust your Spirit to come now and make us new. In Jesus' name, we pray. Amen.

Opening Prayer

Father in heaven, we give you praise and thank you for your Word. You know our hearts, strengths, and wounds, and you judge us rightly because you love us. Use this day—its joys and sufferings—to call us back to you. Let every moment remind us of your goodness, our need for you, and how deeply we belong to you. In Jesus' name, we pray. Amen.

Reflection with Scripture

☐ 1. In Isaiah 28, we hear a warning to the "drunkards of Ephraim." Fr. Mike talks about the grave sin of drunkenness as it can darken the intellect, weaken the will, and increase the attraction to sin. Do I seek to dull my senses through food, drink, or other pleasures in order to cope with something or someone that is difficult for me? How can I better enter into reality and seek God instead?

☐ 2. We can be tempted to view what the prophets say in a purely historical sense. Yet their words can shed light on our spiritual needs, as well. How can we be open to what the prophets are saying when it may affect us spiritually?

☐ 3. Fr. Mike reminds us that often our sins do not end with us. Criticism and rebellion are examples of sins that have far-reaching effects. Is there a time I saw these effects clearly? How can I take steps to halt the harmful effects of sinful choices I have made?

☐ 4. In Zephaniah 3:5, we hear about shamelessness. Do we feel shame for our sins? Though shame is uncomfortable, how can it be helpful? When we are tempted to hide in the shame of our sins, how can we allow that shame to propel us to turn to God's mercy instead?

☐ 5. Baruch begins with the people weeping, fasting, praying, and tithing as they acknowledge their sinfulness (see Baruch 1:5). Why are these actions appropriate in response to sin? How can we increase our sense of urgency to repent of our sins and seek the Sacrament of Reconciliation?

Weekly Challenge

In Isaiah 35, we hear a prophecy of hope, one that ultimately Jesus fulfills. He fulfills many of these prophecies literally so that all can see that he is the Messiah who was prophesied. When John the Baptist was imprisoned and sent messengers to ask Jesus if he is truly the Messiah, Jesus replies with verses from this chapter. This week, take time to read Matthew 11:1–6 and ponder the ways in which Jesus is the fulfillment of Isaiah 35.

Group Activity

In Zephaniah 1, the prophet accuses Judah of five things that strike at their relationship with God: idol worship, failure to pray, poor leadership, superstition, and disbelief in coming judgment. Reflect with your group on how these may also be true for us today— and how they can damage our relationship with the Lord. Then, discuss the remedies: what practical steps can we take to reject these attitudes and grow in faith, prayer, and trust in God's justice and mercy?

Note of Hope

When we feel the depth and shame of sin, we know we have a loving Savior to run to. Our shame is wiped away through his sacrifice on the Cross, and we are given new hope and new life in the glory of his Resurrection. We know that in a life of love with him, these words are true: "From misery to misery we go from mercy to mercy."[6]

Prayer Intentions

Response (R): Your Word, O Lord, is as sweet as honey.

We pray for all missionaries who go to the ends of the earth to spread your Good News: *R.*

We pray for all pastors, who proclaim your holy Word each day: *R.*

We pray for all religious orders to stay close to you always: *R.*

We pray for all religious leaders to stay true to your Word: *R.*

For us, in this year spent with your Word, we pray: *R.*

SCRIPTURE VERSE TO REMEMBER

"Look toward the east, O Jerusalem,
and see the joy that is coming to you from God!"
BARUCH 4:36

---

6. Jean C. J. d'Elbée, *I Believe in Love: A Personal Retreat Based on the Teaching of St. Thérèse of Lisieux* (Manchester, NH: Sophia Institute Press, 2001), 65.

Catechism Connection

These paragraphs in the *Catechism* may be helpful for reflection on the Scripture read this week in *The Bible in a Year*: CCC 756, 1430, 1805

St. Camillus de Lellis, pray for us and all in need, especially the sick, hospital workers, and nurses.
Feast Day: July 18

Highlight from the *Catechism*:

- "There are four virtues that play a pivotal role and accordingly are called 'cardinal'; all the others are grouped around them. They are: prudence, justice, fortitude, and temperance" (CCC 1805).

Closing Prayer

Father in heaven, we give you praise and thank you. You want us to be like your Son, but we go astray and don't love as Christ loves. Send your Spirit into our hearts, for we can't love or live as Christ on our own. With your help, we can do all things. Send your Holy Spirit that we may be fully yours and images of you in this world. In Jesus' name, we pray. Amen.

Opening Prayer

Father in heaven, we give you praise and thank you for being with us in our battles, trials, and sufferings. You are with us every day. Help us when we turn away to come back to you. Help us repent and trust your love and grace, especially when we are confused and don't know where to turn. Help us turn to you this day and every day. In Jesus' name, we pray. Amen.

Reflection with Scripture

☐ 1. As we recall that many of the events recorded in Isaiah take place before the Exile, how does God's promise of fidelity have even more impact? In our own lives, how can we trust in his promise that no matter what happens in the future, he has called us by name?

☐ 2. In chapter 44, Isaiah speaks of how we can turn unremarkable things that we use every day into idols. While we do not often see physical, carved idols around us, are there things in our lives that are taking the place of God? Are there things in our culture that seem benign but are leading to destruction? How can we be more aware of these things and turn back to God in our lives and our culture?

☐ 3. Through God's instructions, Ezekiel condemns the false prophets in chapter 13 of the book of Ezekiel. When we speak, are we, like the false prophets, saying just what is on our minds, or are we speaking with the mind of God? Are we telling people only what they want to hear, or are we saying what they need to hear? Are we ourselves choosing to hear only what we want to hear, or are we choosing to hear what we need to hear?

☐ 4. The Suffering Servant that Isaiah speaks of in Isaiah 50–53 points to Jesus. What stands out to you the most when you meditate on Jesus' suffering through the lens of Isaiah's Suffering Servant?

☐ 5. Isaiah 54:5 speaks of God as a husband to Israel. If someone asked me who my greatest love is, would I respond, "God"? Do I treat my spouse with the kind of love and care that God offers to me?

Weekly Challenge
Read Isaiah 54:10 and reflect on God's mercy. Then write a note of love and gratitude to God, "who has compassion on you." Think about the ways God has given you peace. Pray before you begin writing, asking the Holy Spirit to be with you. After writing it, spend some time in silence to listen to his response.

Group Activity
With your group, divide a large sheet of paper in half from top to bottom, and list the attributes of the Suffering Servant on the left side of the page. Together, think of the ways that the Passion of Jesus fulfilled this prophecy, and list them on the right side of the page. Discuss how Jesus' clear fulfillment of the Suffering Servant prophecy can impact our faith. Conclude by praying the Chaplet of Divine Mercy together.

Note of Hope

Jesus, the Suffering Servant, is merciful. He is trustworthy. Jesus Christ is worthy of our time and our honor and our love. Following his Way, which is Truth and leads to Life, means he must be at the core of our very lives. With Jesus, we enter into a life of mercy and love, a way that brings with it deep peace, joy, and eternal life.

SCRIPTURE VERSE TO REMEMBER

"But now thus says the LORD, he who created you, O Jacob, he who formed you, O Israel: 'Fear not, for I have redeemed you; I have called you by name, you are mine.'"
ISAIAH 43:1

Prayer Intentions

Response (R): You have called us by name, we are yours.
Keep us ever-faithful to your commands: *R.*
Give us strength when we are weary from life's burdens: *R.*
Help us realize the profound love you have for us: *R.*
If we are tempted to worship idols, let us always remember: *R.*
We pray for all priests, who bring us your mercy and take away the weight of sin through the Sacrament of Reconciliation: *R.*
In this year spent with your Word, let us remember: *R.*

St. Mary Magdalene, pray for us and all in need, especially penitent sinners, women, and those in contemplative life.
Feast Day: July 22

Catechism Connection

These paragraphs in the *Catechism* may be helpful for reflection on the Scripture read this week in *The Bible in a Year*: CCC 104, 601, 755, 982

Highlight from the *Catechism*:

- "There is no offense, however serious, that the Church cannot forgive. 'There is no one, however wicked and guilty, who may not confidently hope for forgiveness, provided his repentance is honest.' Christ who died for all men desires that in his Church the gates of forgiveness should always be open to anyone who turns away from sin" (CCC 982).

Closing Prayer

Father in heaven, we give you praise and glory. Every day you bring us to hear your Word, which is living and effective and accomplishes your will. We are grateful. Please help us say yes to your will and your Word this day and every day. In Jesus' name, we pray. Amen.

Reflection with Scripture

☐ 1. A common theme of Ezekiel is that idolatry is often represented as adultery. Fr. Mike reminds us that idolatry means taking good things and making them ultimate things. How can we purify our hearts and our relationship with God by the proper use of things?

☐ 2. We hear of Ezekiel's lament as Zedekiah is the last of the kings of the line of David. Afterward, the royal line goes "underground." The people of Israel are waiting, walking in darkness, and wondering how God's promise of a Messiah through the line of David will be fulfilled. Is there something in life that you are waiting for that seems impossible? How do you relate to the Israelites in this longing? What can we learn from God's fulfillment of his promise in Jesus?

☐ 3. Isaiah 61 is what Jesus reads in the synagogue. He proclaims to the people listening, "Today this Scripture has been fulfilled in your hearing" (Luke 4:21). How can we as members of his Mystical Body, the Church, continue to bring the fulfillment of this Scripture passage into the world today?

☐ 4. Fr. Mike reminds us that as Christians we are meant to be "God's mailmen," not his "editors." We must deliver his entire message. Is there a situation where you know someone needs to hear God's full message, but you are tempted to make it "sound better"? What virtues can you pray for to embolden your heart to proclaim God's Good News?

☐ The response of the Ammonites and the Moabites when the Temple is destroyed is wrong. Sometimes, we can have the wrong response: indifference when we encounter beauty, rejoicing when we see something good destroyed, or resentment when others try to build up what is good. What are some ways we can purify our hearts to have a proper response to what is true and good? How can we see our emotions as an important guide but not an exclusive authority?

Weekly Challenge

Take time to reflect on ways you can act with greater wisdom and charity in your relationships. How can you respond to people and situations instead of reacting? How can you ask God to reform and purify your emotions and feelings? What ways can you grow in stronger willpower and discipline? What changes do you need to make to grow?

Group Activity

Isaiah 60 begins, "Arise, shine; for your light has come." Jesus later calls his disciples to be light for the world. Write each group member's name on a slip of paper. Draw names, and on the back, anonymously write one or two talents of that person. Return the slips, shuffle, then hand them to the named individuals. Reflect on the talents received—were any surprising? Then, discuss as a group how to use these gifts to shine Christ's light for others.

Note of Hope

The Lord has given each of us unique talents and gifts. When we use them for his greater glory and the building up of his kingdom, we become lights shining in the darkness. Let us encourage one another to shine brightly, and let us help cultivate one another's gifts through connection, generosity, and joy.

SCRIPTURE VERSE TO REMEMBER

"Before I formed you in the womb I knew you,
and before you were born I consecrated you;
I appointed you a prophet to the nations."
JEREMIAH 1:5

Prayer Intentions

Response (R): Christ, be our light!

When we are tempted to take good things and make them our ultimate things, may we always turn to you instead: *R.*

As we gather the wealth of your Word, little by little: *R.*

As we wait in longing for your return: *R.*

As we continue to be your hands and your feet in the world: *R.*

As we strive to rest and worship well each Sunday: *R.*

In this year spent with your Word: *R.*

St. Martha, pray for us all, especially cooks, housewives, and those who serve others.
Feast Day: July 29

Catechism Connection

These paragraphs in the *Catechism* may be helpful for reflection on the Scripture read this week in *The Bible in a Year*: CCC 763, 1043, 1435

Highlight from the *Catechism*:

- "It was the Son's task to accomplish the Father's plan of salvation in the fullness of time. Its accomplishment was the reason for his being sent. 'The Lord Jesus inaugurated his Church by preaching the Good News, that is, the coming of the Kingdom of God, promised beforehand in the Scriptures'" (CCC 763).

Closing Prayer

Father in heaven, we thank you and give you praise. Thank you for this day and your words. We deserve your justice but need your mercy. You do not delay in judgment; please do not delay in mercy. We have fallen and need your mercy now. Your mercy is new every morning. Help us turn back to you in every way. We pray in Jesus' name. Amen.

Opening Prayer

Father in heaven, we give you praise and thank you for calling us to repent and come back to you. You have a plan for our lives and want us close to you. Even when we fail, you do not abandon us because you are a good Dad. Help us to say yes to your heart and will, and to turn away from what we have trusted instead of you. In Jesus' name, we pray. Amen.

Reflection with Scripture

☐ 1. In Proverbs 14:10, we read, "The heart knows its own bitterness." Do I acknowledge the true motives of my heart? Or do I try to justify my actions when I act, think, or say something unjust or "bitter"?

☐ 2. As we hear Ezekiel 28, we are reminded that we, too, can begin to think that the beauty, position, or wealth God has given us comes from ourselves instead of coming from him as a gift. Fr. Mike reminds us that we can begin to think of these things as our rights instead of as gifts. What are some ways we can remind ourselves that everything we have comes from God?

☐ 3. Jeremiah is known as the "weeping prophet" because he lets his heart be broken. Are we sensitive to the evils of this world? Does sin break our hearts? Or have we hardened our hearts? Why is it important to have a sensitivity to sin?

☐ 4. In Jeremiah 2:32, the prophet speaks of a bride. The Lord is our greatest love. How can we prepare our hearts for him as a bride and groom prepare for their wedding day?

☐ 5. Ezekiel sees a vision of a valley of dried bones. What does this vision point to spiritually? What did the vision symbolize for Israel, and what does it represent for us? When you experience a spiritual season of dryness, do you turn to the Holy Spirit to breathe life into you?

Weekly Challenge

Say a prayer asking God for the grace to share the Faith. This week, be on the lookout for the ways he is calling you to live out your faith and proclaim his Good News by both your words and your actions. Ask for the gifts of courage, fortitude, and joy as you spread his light through your light.

Group Activity

Invite each member of the group to share what spiritual season they are in. Are you in a season of joy? Dryness? Hope? Longing? Waiting? Share any intentions you may have during this season. Then, together, pray to the Holy Spirit.

Note of Hope

It is the Lord who can breathe new life into our dry bones and into our stony, hardened hearts. He alone can give us a new heart, a new spirit. Each day this week is an opportunity, a new beginning in him. Let the Holy Spirit come and breathe new life into you.

SCRIPTURE VERSE TO REMEMBER

*"A new heart I will give you, and a new spirit
I will put within you; and I will take out of your flesh
the heart of stone and give you a heart of flesh."*
EZEKIEL 36:26

Prayer Intentions

Response (R): Holy Spirit, breathe new life into us!
When we experience dryness in our prayer: *R.*
When we are tempted to act with insincerity in our worship of you:
R.
When we realize our heart's bitterness: *R.*
When our hearts are hardened to sin: *R.*
When we need the courage to guard your Word: *R.*
In this year spent with your Word. *R.*

St. John Vianney, pray for us all, especially priests, confessors, and those in pastoral care.
Feast Day: August 4

Catechism **Connection**

These paragraphs in the *Catechism* may be helpful for reflection on the Scripture read this week in *The Bible in a Year*: CCC 210, 450, 896, 1443

Highlight from the *Catechism*:

- "During his public life Jesus not only forgave sins, but also made plain the effect of this forgiveness: he reintegrated forgiven sinners into the community of the People of God from which sin had alienated or even excluded them" (CCC 1443).

Closing Prayer

Father in heaven, we give you praise and glory. You are good, our Father, our Dad. You call us back and conquer death. Send your Holy Spirit—the Spirit that raised Jesus and came upon the apostles—to bring life to the broken, dead, and lost parts of us. Let your Spirit bring us home to you. We ask this in Jesus' name. Amen.

Opening Prayer

Father in heaven, we give you praise and glory. Watch over our words, thoughts, and hearts, Lord, for we are good but broken. Fill our minds with your Truth, our hearts with your love, and guide our mouths to speak only what builds up and helps others. Touch us with your Spirit so we reflect your truth and love. In Jesus' name, we pray. Amen.

Reflection with Scripture

☐ 1. How do we respond when we see injustice? It is easy to feel angry, but often we stop there. How can we let our hearts be propelled into movement and action like the prophet Jeremiah?

☐ 2. Do we put our trust in wisdom, might, or riches? How can we guard against doing so and instead, as we hear in Jeremiah 9, glory in God's steadfast love, justice, and righteousness?

☐ 3. In Proverbs 15, we hear how the foolish do not desire to be reproved, taught, or corrected. Fr. Mike explains how the opposite of foolishness is a docile heart, a heart that can be taught. The word "docility" comes from the Latin *docilitatem*, meaning "teachableness." In what ways can we grow in the virtue of docility?

☐ 4. In Jeremiah 14, we hear about false prophets. Are there people that we follow who may speak eloquently, and who say compelling words we like to hear, but are not speaking truth? How can we guard against the "false prophets" in our lives?

☐ 5. During the Exile, Daniel and his three companions only ate food that was permissible according to the Law. During difficult times, do I use the difficulty as an excuse not to follow God's commandments? Or do I strive to follow his commands no matter the situation?

Weekly Challenge

Ezekiel 47 speaks of water flowing toward the east from the Temple. This foreshadows the blood and water that flowed from the side of Jesus when he was pierced on the Cross (see John 19:34). This week, find a crucifix, or an image of the Crucifixion, and take time to pray and ponder in front of it. Thank God for the gift of his sacrifice. Spend time in silence listening to what he has to tell you through this image of his great love for you.

Group Activity

Ezekiel 46:9 says, "He who enters by the north gate to worship shall go out by the south gate ... no one shall return by way of the gate by which he entered." This points to the transformation that should happen each time we attend Mass. As a group, discuss: Do we allow God to change us through each sacrifice of the Mass? How can we support one another in being transformed so that we never leave worship the same way we arrived?

Note of Hope

In the noise of this world, we have the stillness and beauty of the Host, Jesus in the Eucharist. The Mass offers many things to us: a time of rest and renewal, a time of worship, participation in a great feast, teachable moments, and the opportunity to glory in God's love. May we enter more deeply into the elements of the Mass, giving God thanks for all these beautiful gifts.

SCRIPTURE VERSE TO REMEMBER

"Better is a little with the fear of the Lord than great treasure and trouble with it."
PROVERBS 15:16

Prayer Intentions

Response (R): Lord, you are the Way, the Truth, and the Life!

Help us turn from the false prophets of the world and seek you: **R.**

Help us forgive when someone has broken our trust: **R.**

Help us repent if we break someone's trust: **R.**

Help us have a docile heart for you to teach and form: **R.**

Help us be cheerful in anticipation of your Great Heavenly Feast: **R.**

Help us in this year spent with your Word: **R.**

Catechism Connection

These paragraphs in the *Catechism* may be helpful for reflection on the Scripture read this week in *The Bible in a Year*: CCC 64, 272, 429, 1042

St. Jane Frances de Chantal, pray for us and all in need, especially widows, the sick, and the poor.
Feast Day: August 12

Highlight from the *Catechism*:

- "At the end of time, the Kingdom of God will come in its fullness. After the universal judgment, the righteous will reign forever with Christ, glorified in body and soul. The universe itself will be renewed" (CCC 1042).

Closing Prayer

Father in heaven, we thank you and give you praise and glory. Thank you for helping us follow Jeremiah, the weeping prophet, and for introducing us to Daniel and his companions. We thank you for the gift of these prophets who point us to your Truth. Help us to walk and live in your Truth this day and every day. In Jesus' name, we pray. Amen.

Opening Prayer

Father in heaven, we thank you and give you praise and glory. Thank you for your Word and for revealing your heart to us. Please help our hearts to receive you, hear you, and be more like you. Help us to love what you love and be in your image so others may see you in us. We pray in Jesus' name. Amen.

Reflection with Scripture

☐ 1. One of the ways that Jeremiah tells King Shallum that he must reform is by helping the poor. In paragraph 2405, the *Catechism* tells us that, "Those who hold goods for use and consumption should use them with moderation, reserving the better part for guests, for the sick and the poor." Are these words surprising? Are there things we need to change about our lifestyle to live these words out to the fullest?

☐ 2. Hananiah, Azariah, and Mishael refuse to worship the idol that King Nebuchadnezzar erected. In anger, the King says he will throw them into a fiery furnace. Their response shows great trust. Often in prayer we place constraints and conditions on our trust in God. How can the story of the fiery furnace help us to follow God's will, no matter the outcome?

☐ 3. When God protected Daniel from the lions, Daniel was able to proclaim his innocence (see Daniel 6:22). Again, in Daniel 13, we hear about how Susanna is wrongfully accused. What is the impact of wrongful accusation? How can we be more prudent in our speech and our thoughts so that we do not jump to conclusions about others and also do not turn a blind eye to wrongdoing? Do we realize the seriousness and weight of making accusations?

☐ 4. When the world around us seems unstable, how can we better rely on the stability of "the one that was ancient of days" (Daniel 7:9)?

☐ 5. Do we submit to God's commandments as if they were the "wooden bars" of a yoke? Or do we resist the commandments to the point where we are given "bars of iron" instead, as Jeremiah 28:13 says?

Weekly Challenge

Take time to ponder the beginning of Susanna's prayer in Daniel 13, as she speaks to God, who knows all things. Reflect on these words and ask God to bring to light anything in your heart that needs his light. Pray and ask him for a greater trust in him, who knows all things before they even come about.

Group Activity

As a group, discuss if your relationship with God the Father has changed since starting *The Bible in a Year* podcast. If it has, describe in what ways it has. If it hasn't, share what your relationship is like with him right now. How has listening to the Old Testament and Fr. Mike's reflections impacted your relationships with others?

Note of Hope

Our life story is about realizing how loved we are by God, accepting that love, and in turn, extending that same love to others. When we experience the powerful love of God, we in turn desire to love more. God's love humbles us. It makes us live more intimately with the rest of humanity, just as Christ did in his Incarnation. He is Love. May we have the courage to accept his love and the wisdom to realize that we are his.

SCRIPTURE VERSE TO REMEMBER

"You will seek me and find me;
when you seek me with all your heart."
JEREMIAH 29:13

Prayer Intentions

Response (R): Lord, we seek you with all our hearts.
We pray for all those who are wrongfully accused, that truth may reign: *R.*
We pray for all those who bravely defend those who are accused wrongfully: *R.*
We pray that we may always use our goods in moderation so as to better serve the poor: *R.*
We pray for a greater boldness to proclaim you publicly: *R.*
We pray that you transform our arrogance into humility: *R.*
We pray for help to submit humbly to your yoke of love: *R.*
In this year spent with your Word: *R.*

St. Pius X, pray for us all, especially first communicants and those who promote the Eucharist.
Feast Day: August 21

Catechism Connection

These paragraphs in the *Catechism* may be helpful for reflection on the Scripture read this week in *The Bible in a Year*: CCC 269, 305, 1866, 2540

Highlight from the *Catechism*:

- "Jesus asks for childlike abandonment to the providence of our heavenly Father who takes care of his children's smallest needs: 'Therefore do not be anxious, saying, "What shall we eat?" or "What shall we drink?" ... Your heavenly Father knows that you need them all'" (CCC 305).

Closing Prayer

Father in heaven, we give you praise and glory. Thank you for this day and for the book of Daniel. Thank you for bringing us to this moment. God, you are with us through everything—distress, tornadoes, storms of life. Please remind us of your presence this day and every day. In Jesus' name, we pray. Amen.

Opening Prayer

Father in heaven, we give you praise and thank you for your Word, the prophet Jeremiah, and Judith. Thank you for your wisdom and your will that calls us to walk daily. Help us to live this day in your hands, heart, and will, saying yes to you in all we plan and do. In Jesus' name, we pray. Amen.

Reflection with Scripture

☐ 1. As we hear the words of Jeremiah 32, Fr. Mike shares the truth that "God doesn't resent you for needing his forgiveness." How do these words impact you? Do you believe the lie that God resents you? Or do you believe that God rejoices in being your Savior?

☐ 2. As we hear that Jeremiah remains in prison, we are reminded that God's silence does not mean he is absent. What actions can we take to renew our trust when we are tempted to think he is not listening to our prayers?

☐ 3. As we hear about the faithfulness of the Rechabites in Jeremiah 35, we are challenged to see that often we see ourselves as heroic in our faith for having morals that are just slightly better than the standard that is prevalent in our society. However, when we surround ourselves with morally upright and noble people, we realize that God is calling us higher. Who or what is the true standard for holiness? Is it society? Or is it God and his saints?

☐ 4. When Jeremiah's words that God speaks to him are brought to King Jehoiakim on a scroll, the king starts cutting sections of the scroll out and throwing them into the fire (see Jeremiah 36:23). Do I "cut out" and dismiss the parts of Scripture or Church teaching that feel too difficult for me?

☐ 5. Jeremiah is a prophet who foreshadows Christ's suffering for us, as he allowed himself to suffer with the people. Do we avoid suffering at all costs, even the cost of our own and others' holiness? How can we take steps to accept the suffering God allows for us?

Weekly Challenge

In Proverbs 17:9, we hear about harmful words. This week, reflect on how you speak to those closest to you: your family, your friends, and your coworkers. How can you guard and purify your speech this week? Does everything you say need to be said? Do you bring up past faults too often? Challenge yourself to speak words of the Spirit: love, joy, peace, patience, kindness, goodness, and self-control.

Group Activity

Proverbs 17:3 says, "The LORD tries hearts." We all face difficult moments. Invite group members to reflect on any challenges they're currently facing. Discuss how trials can purify our hearts like gold in a furnace, and how we might see suffering as refinement. Then pray together using Fr. Mike's words: "Yes, Lord, I know in this moment you're working with me, and I know that you can do all things. I know that you can work all things for good for those who love you."

Note of Hope

Each difficulty is an opportunity to be refined by the Lord in the fire of his love. When we encounter struggles this week, may we ask God to purify our hearts and form them in the divine furnace of his love. He knows what we need. Let us entrust our hearts to him that he can mold and shape us into the saints he desires us to become!

SCRIPTURE VERSE TO REMEMBER

"For your power depends not upon numbers, nor your might upon men of strength; for you are God of the lowly, helper of the oppressed, upholder of the weak, protector of the forlorn, savior of those without hope."
JUDITH 9:11

Prayer Intentions

Response (R): Refine and purify our hearts, O God!

We pray for all marriages and families, that they may reflect the love and sacrifice you have for your Bride, the Church: **R.**

We pray for those whose hearts have been broken and misused, that they may find comfort in your most Sacred Heart: **R.**

We pray for those we have hurt by acting in anger: **R.**

We pray for the grace to acknowledge our faults and turn to you in repentance: **R.**

We pray for an end to all violence and abuse: **R.**

In this year spent with your Word: **R.**

St. Monica, pray for us all, especially mothers and wives.
Feast Day: August 27

Catechism Connection

These paragraphs in the *Catechism* may be helpful for reflection on the Scripture read this week in *The Bible in a Year*: CCC 307, 1432, 2563

Highlight from the *Catechism*:

- "To human beings God even gives the power of freely sharing in his providence by entrusting them with the responsibility of 'subduing' the earth and having dominion over it. God thus enables men to be intelligent and free causes in order to complete the work of creation" (CCC 307).

Closing Prayer

Father in heaven, we thank you for your Word, your will, and your heart. Thank you for this journey and for giving us perseverance to keep listening. We thank you for Jeremiah, who faithfully spoke your Word even when unpopular. Thank you for giving him as a witness to encourage us as we race toward your Son, Jesus Christ. In Jesus' name, we pray. Amen.

Reflection with Scripture

☐ 1. As we reflect on the Lamentations of Jeremiah, do we, like him, allow our pain to become a prayer? Do we see suffering as an opportunity to bring more prayer to the Lord?

☐ 2. In Proverbs 18:2, we hear, "A fool takes no pleasure in understanding, but only in expressing his opinion." When we communicate with others, are we expressing our opinions more than we are seeking to understand others' thoughts and needs? How would seeking to understand improve our current relationships?

☐ 3. As we hear some of the final chapters in Jeremiah, we are challenged to recognize that the words of the prophets are for us, not just for Jeremiah's contemporaries. Do I rebel against the Lord through my indifference? Through taking him for granted? Or by being selective with his commands?

☐ 4. Reflecting on Lamentations, Fr. Mike shares that "suffering has the ability to purify us and make us better, but it also has the ability to reveal the darkness and brokenness of our own hearts." What do we need to do to allow suffering to purify us, not to make us bitter?

☐ 5. How is your heart impacted when you hear Jesus' genealogy filled not only with virtuous people but also with people who have done gravely sinful things? Do you see beauty and hope in this?

Weekly Challenge

Take time this week to reflect on the visit of the Wise Men in the second chapter of Matthew. Ponder the last verse of the story, where we are told that the Wise Men took "another way" to get home (see Matthew 2:12). How has your own encounter with the Person of Jesus left you changed? Experiencing the Person of Jesus causes us to choose "another way"—a different way to live. Pick one thing to do this week to reflect the light of Jesus to those who encounter you, so that they, too, have the opportunity to be changed by encountering him.

Group Activity

The prophets brought God's Word to others. As a group, set aside time to write notes of encouragement to friends or family. Encourage group members to help each other find Bible verses to include with the notes.

Note of Hope

When Jesus called his first disciples, they immediately left their nets and followed him (see Matthew 4:20). They encountered Christ in a powerful way. We, too, can encounter him and belong to his Body, the Church. When we choose him above all else, our lives become truly blessed. That's when we begin walking in the footsteps of the saints. May we have the courage to follow him each day.

SCRIPTURE VERSE TO REMEMBER

"Let your light so shine before men, that they may see your good works and give glory to your Father who is in heaven."
MATTHEW 5:16

Prayer Intentions

Response (R): With all God's people, we cry out, Lord, hear our prayer!
For all the vulnerable who are neglected and uncared for, may they feel the loving presence of Christ and his Mother: *R.*
That each day we, with all the members of the Church, may enter into a deeper conversion of heart: *R.*
That we may allow our suffering to purify our hearts: *R.*
That we may allow our pain to become prayer: *R.*
That we, like the Wise Men, may allow ourselves to depart a different way when we encounter the Person of Christ: *R.*
In this year spent with your Word: *R.*

St. Gregory the Great, patron saint of musicians and singers, pray for us.
Feast Day: September 3

Catechism Connection

These paragraphs in the *Catechism* may be helpful for reflection on the Scripture read this week in *The Bible in a Year*: CCC 1038, 2546, 410, 1820, 2648

Highlight from the *Catechism*:

- "Every joy and suffering, every event and need can become the matter for thanksgiving which, sharing in that of Christ, should fill one's whole life: 'Give thanks in all circumstances' (1 Thess 5:18)" (CCC 2648).

Closing Prayer

Father in heaven, we give you praise. Thank you for teaching us to call you Father. We thank you for the Gospel of Matthew and for those who handed down your Word by the Spirit through the Church. Help us to allow your Word to transform our lives. In Jesus' name, we pray. Amen.

Opening Prayer

Father in heaven, we give you praise. Thank you for your Word and for revealing Jesus through the Gospels. Thank you for calling Matthew and inspiring him to write these words. Help us never to wander from you, but to choose your will and follow you with our whole heart. Help us to love you fully. In Jesus' name, we pray. Amen.

Reflection with Scripture

☐ 1. Reflecting on Matthew 10:32, what are ways we acknowledge our faithfulness to Jesus before others? Some ideas include praying grace before meals in restaurants or asking to pray with people who are going through something difficult. Do the people we encounter each day know that we believe in and love Jesus?

☐ 2. When Jesus walks on the sea, the disciples cry out in fear. Jesus responds, "Take heart, it is I; have no fear" (Matthew 14:27). Is there a situation that I am undergoing right now in which Jesus is saying these same words to me?

☐ 3. Jesus tells his disciples, "Unless you turn and become like children, you will never enter the kingdom of heaven" (Matthew 18:13). How can we become more childlike so as to enter his kingdom?

☐ 4. When Jesus encounters the rich young man and invites him to be a disciple, the man leaves in sadness due to his riches (see Matthew 19:16–22). Jesus is asking the same of us: to follow him. Would we walk away sorrowful because we cling to our possessions? Or would we follow him joyfully? What path do we choose each day?

☐ 5. In what ways do I relate to Peter when he denies Jesus during his Passion? How can I turn in hope back toward God when I betray him?

Weekly Challenge

Peter declared Jesus as the Christ in Matthew 16. Reflect on G. K. Chesterton's words from *Heretics*: "Christ … chose for his cornerstone … a shuffler, a snob, a coward—in a word, a man. And upon this rock he has built his Church … All the empires … failed … founded by strong men … But this one thing … was founded on a weak man, and for that reason it is indestructible. For no chain is stronger than its weakest link."[7] What insights or thoughts do you have regarding G. K. Chesterton's words?

Group Activity

As Matthew was writing his Gospel to a Jewish audience, the Old Testament was important to those who first heard his Gospel account. Discuss how reading the Old Testament has helped prepare you for the Gospel of Matthew. Share the ways that it has opened up Matthew and has enriched the stories for you. Take turns sharing which part of Matthew's Gospel impacted you the most, and why.

_____

7. G. K. Chesterton, *Heretics* (Irvine, CA: Xist Classics, 2016).

Note of Hope

Jesus is the Bridegroom of our hearts. He came to save us from the consequences of sin and death. Not only does he want to be our Savior, but he also desires to be our friend. May we always see him as our best friend and our greatest love. May we grow in friendship and love with him each day, so as to make his kingdom come alive here on earth.

SCRIPTURE VERSE TO REMEMBER

"Truly I say to you, unless you turn and become like children, you will never enter the kingdom of heaven."
MATTHEW 18:3

Prayer Intentions

Response (R): God of our salvation, hear and answer us.
We pray for all those preparing to enter our Church: *R.*
We pray that you always remain the greatest love of our hearts: *R.*
We pray that we may become like little children so as to enter your kingdom joyfully: *R.*
We pray for our Holy Father the Pope and for all bishops: *R.*
In this year spent with your Word: *R.*

St. Peter Claver, pray for us and all in need, especially those evangelizing enslaved people.
Feast Day: September 9

Catechism Connection

These paragraphs in the *Catechism* may be helpful for reflection on the Scripture read this week in *The Bible in a Year*: CCC 536, 546, 1431, 1716, 2843

Highlight from the *Catechism*:

- "Interior repentance is a radical reorientation of our whole life, a return, a conversion to God with all our heart, an end of sin, a turning away from evil, with repugnance toward the evil actions we have committed. At the same time it entails the desire and resolution to change one's life, with hope in God's mercy and trust in the help of his grace" (CCC 1431).

Closing Prayer

Father in heaven, we give you praise. We thank you for the Passion, Death, and Resurrection of your Son, and for the Spirit that raised him, given to us in Baptism. Help us to obey Jesus' command to go and make disciples, sharing your love, power, and goodness. Thank you for all you do in our lives. In Jesus' name, we pray. Amen.

Opening Prayer

Father in heaven, we give you praise and thanks. Thank you for reminding us, like the people of Israel, that we are made for two worlds—this life and the eternal home. Help us to long for that true home, to live with hope, and to be faithful until you bring us there by your grace. In Jesus' name, we pray. Amen.

Reflection with Scripture

☐ 1. In the first chapter of the book of Haggai, we hear an invitation to reflection. How often do we take time to reflect on what has happened in our lives? Why is it important to examine our lives? How can we do this more regularly, such as by making a habit each evening of daily reflection and examination of conscience?

☐ 2. As the book of Ezra begins, we hear that worship is restored in Jerusalem and the foundation of the Temple is being laid. As the people see this, they begin to weep because the foundation is smaller than the original glorious Temple of Solomon. We, too, can get stuck looking back at the past instead of praising God for the gift of the present. What actions can we take to firmly root ourselves in the present moment?

☐ 3. In Ezra 7:10 we hear that Ezra "had set his heart to study the law of the LORD." Do we prioritize the study of the law of the Lord in our life? Do we set our heart on the law of the Lord or things of this world?

☐ 4. In Zechariah 12:10, we hear the prophecy about Jesus on the Cross: "When they look on him whom they have pierced, they shall mourn for him." When we see a crucifix or reflect on Jesus' Passion, do we mourn? Have we become indifferent to his suffering? What is the right response to seeing our Lord and Savior, our greatest Love, suffering on the Cross?

☐ 5. In the third chapter of the book of Nehemiah, we hear how people come together to work in partnership to rebuild the walls of Jerusalem. In what ways can we be more open to working together to build up our Church?

Weekly Challenge

This week, reflect on Zechariah 3:9 and how Jesus removed our guilt. Invite a friend to join you in a sacrifice this Friday. Together, come up with an intention to sacrifice for. Help encourage one another to keep the sacrifice through prayer.

Group Activity

As a group, discuss the importance of acts of penance, specifically the Church's call for fasting and abstinence. Share ways that you can keep one another accountable and encouraged in your acts of penance.

Note of Hope

Each sacrifice we make, though we may not realize or see it in the moment, has everlasting and eternal effects. United in the Communion of Saints, each sacrifice we make builds up and strengthens the Church, the Bride and Body of Christ. No sacrifice of yours is forgotten or overlooked by the Good Father. Rather, each sacrifice, no matter how small, is lovingly united to his.

SCRIPTURE VERSE TO REMEMBER

"Do not say, 'I will repay evil';
wait for the LORD, and he will help you."
PROVERBS 20:22

Prayer Intentions

Response (R): Stay with us, Lord.

When we reflect on our life and ponder how you are always with us: *R.*

When we feel apathy enter into our hearts: *R.*

When we offer thanksgiving for the guilt you have removed from our hearts: *R.*

As we gaze in love upon you, the Pierced One: *R.*

When we set our hearts upon the study of your laws: *R.*

In this year spent with your Word: *R.*

St. Robert Bellarmine, pray for catechists, for theologians, and for us all. **Feast Day: September 17**

Catechism Connection

These paragraphs in the *Catechism* may be helpful for reflection on the Scripture read this week in *The Bible in a Year*: CCC 1180, 2037, 2046

Highlight from the *Catechism*:

- "By living with the mind of Christ, Christians *hasten the coming of the Reign of God,* 'a kingdom of justice, love and peace.' They do not, for all that, abandon their earthly tasks; faithful to their master, they fulfill them with uprightness, patience, and love" (CCC 2046).

Closing Prayer

Father in heaven, we praise and thank you for your goodness and love. You call us to build your kingdom where we are, to be temples and agents of your Holy Spirit. Help us bring your light, love, hope, mercy, truth, and justice into our corners of the world. May your voice be heard and your will be done. In Jesus' name, we pray. Amen.

Reflection with Scripture

☐ 1. Nehemiah and those rebuilding the walls of Jerusalem faced great opposition in their work. In response, Nehemiah prayed and took action (see Nehemiah 4:9). Do we do our part and take action when we need to? Do we pray? What steps can we take to remember to combine prayer and action?

☐ 2. Men plotting against Nehemiah tell him to meet them in one of the villages. Nehemiah responds, "I am doing a great work and I cannot come down" (Nehemiah 6:3). Do we respond in the same way when others try to distract us from our vocations and work? Or do we seek out distractions throughout the day?

☐ 3. When Nehemiah, Ezra, and the Levites proclaim the Law of the Lord, the people weep (see Nehemiah 8:9). What do you think moved their hearts so deeply? Their weeping reflects that they have a relationship with God and are reminded of the covenant they have with him. Do we allow God to pierce our hearts with his loving and merciful Word?

☐ 4. In response to their weeping, Nehemiah tells the people to celebrate. He instructs them, saying, "The joy of the LORD is your strength" (Nehemiah 8:10). How is joy related to strength?

☐ 5. Esther asks for the intercession of the people through fasting before she goes to the king (see Esther 4:16). When we are in need of prayers, do we ask for people to intercede for us? What can we learn from the humility and trust of Esther regarding intercessory prayer?

Weekly Challenge

Pray a Rosary this week and reflect on Queen Esther, who foreshadows Mother Mary and her intercession for us, her children. Before you begin, ask the Holy Spirit to place a person or a situation on your heart that needs Mother Mary's intercession, and ask her help through the prayer of the Rosary.

Group Activity

Esther 4:14 says, "Who knows whether you have not come to the kingdom for such a time as this?" God raises up people with unique gifts for a specific time and mission. Choose three saints from different eras, prepare brief bios and backgrounds, and display their images. Invite group members to read and discuss each saint's historical impact. Then reflect: How might God be calling you to be a light in this moment in history? What is your mission today?

Note of Hope

The Lord has placed you in a specific place, in a specific time. He has woven you beautifully in the tapestry of his plan. You are sent into the world with a mission to allow him to love you and in turn, love him through your love of others. Do not be afraid to boldly live out your call, the mission he has entrusted you with.

SCRIPTURE VERSE TO REMEMBER

"The spirit of man is the lamp of the LORD, searching all his innermost parts."
PROVERBS 20:27

Prayer Intentions

Response (R): Grant our prayer according to your will, O Lord.

That we may turn to you in prayer and take action when we need to: **R.**

For your grace when we are tempted to wander away from the duties of our vocation: **R.**

That your joy may always be our strength: **R.**

That we may always intercede for those in need: **R.**

For work for the unemployed, those seeking employment, and those facing difficulties within their jobs: **R.**

For guidance for those who hold roles in public office: **R.**

For perseverance in this year spent with your Word: **R.**

Catechism Connection

These paragraphs in the *Catechism* may be helpful for reflection on the Scripture read this week in *The Bible in a Year*: CCC 1434, 1808, 2101, 2637

St. Pius of Pietrelcina (Padre Pio), pray for stress relief for us all, for adolescents, and for those suffering physical pain.
Feast Day: September 23

Highlight from the *Catechism*:

- "*Fortitude* is the moral virtue that ensures firmness in difficulties and constancy in the pursuit of the good. It strengthens the resolve to resist temptations and to overcome obstacles in the moral life. The virtue of fortitude enables one to conquer fear, even fear of death, and to face trials and persecutions" (CCC 1808).

Closing Prayer

Father in heaven, we praise you and thank you for your Word and your faithful presence with your chosen people. Send your Holy Spirit upon us so we may know we are chosen, loved, and covenanted to you. Help us always live as your children, confident that you are our Father now and forever. We thank and praise you. In Jesus' name, we pray. Amen.

Reflection with Scripture

☐ 1. In Malachi 3:1, we hear a prophecy pointing forward to John the Baptist, who was called by God "to prepare the way" (see Matthew 3:3). How can we prepare the way among those we encounter to help them open their minds and hearts to the Gospel?

☐ 2. 1 Maccabees begins with persecution of the Jewish people by the Seleucid Empire under Antiochus Epiphanes' rule. We read in 1 Maccabees 1:41–42 that Antiochus Epiphanes demanded that each Jewish person "give up his customs." How can we hold onto and practice the traditions and customs of our Faith in the midst of a culture that tells us to abandon them?

☐ 3. The last words of the faithful Mattathias to his sons entreat them to "Remember the deeds of the fathers": Abraham, Joseph, Phinehas, Joshua, Caleb, David, and Daniel (see 1 Maccabees 2:51–60). What can we learn from this example of looking back on the lives of the faithfully departed as a source of strength? Do we do the same with the lives of the saints, including the ones Mattathias listed?

☐ 4. Sirach 11 reminds us not to judge solely based on outward appearance (see Sirach 11:4). Why are we so tempted to judge others based on their appearance? How can we approach others as a mystery and a gift?

☐ 5. In 1 Maccabees 3:19, Judas encourages the people by proclaiming, "Strength comes from Heaven." So often, we are disheartened by our weakness. How does this verse encourage us to depend on the strength of heaven throughout the challenges we face each day?

Weekly Challenge
One of the vices Malachi points out is the corruption of the priesthood. This week, pray each day for all priests. You can pray from your heart or use "St. Thérèse of Lisieux's Prayer for Priests," available for free on AscensionPress.com.

Group Activity
In the beginning of 1 Maccabees, we hear about Mattathias and his sons, who stood firm despite persecution. Around the world, many Christians are persecuted in the present day. As a group, pray the Chaplet of Divine Mercy for those who are in danger because of their faith.

Note of Hope

God delights in us and in his saints, his Creation. He finds pleasure in us seeking the intercession and the guidance of his saints, the men and women who have run the race and now wear their crown of glory—a crown we eagerly await. Let us call upon their powerful intercession, those men, women, and children who behold the Face of Christ in Beatitude. May we be counted among them some day!

SCRIPTURE VERSE TO REMEMBER

"It is not on the size of the army that victory in battle depends, but strength comes from Heaven."
1 MACCABEES 3:19

Prayer Intentions

Response (R): The Lord is compassionate and merciful, for as his majesty is, so also is his mercy.

Replace our judgmental, stony hearts with hearts of love: **R.**

Grant us the grace to use the virtue of prudence in forming friendships: **R.**

Grant us the strength to avoid every near occasion of sin: **R.**

We pray for all priests, especially those who are in most need of your mercy: **R.**

In this year spent with your Word, let us remember each day: **R.**

Catechism Connection

These paragraphs in the *Catechism* may be helpful for reflection on the Scripture read this week in *The Bible in a Year*: CCC 227, 1807, 1816

Highlight from the *Catechism*:

- "*Justice* is the moral virtue that consists in the constant and firm will to give their due to God and neighbor. Justice toward God is called the 'virtue of religion'" (CCC 1807).

Closing Prayer

Father in heaven, we thank you for your Word and for unfolding the history of Israel before us. Thank you for the Wisdom of Ben Sira (the book of Sirach). Please grant us your grace each day, that we may belong to you and glorify you in all we do. In Jesus' name, we pray. Amen.

Reflection with Scripture

☐ 1. The book of Maccabees is filled with stories of battles. What can we learn from these battles for our daily spiritual battles?

☐ 2. Sirach 23:18 speaks about the tendency to think our sins are hidden. So often, we think that our personal sin doesn't affect anyone else, yet sin truly affects the entire Body of Christ. We do not want our private sins to become public. Which do we desire more: not to get caught in our sin or not to sin at all?

☐ 3. In Maccabees 10, the Jewish people do not trust Demetrius' bribe because he has not kept his past promises. According to Fr. Gregory Pine, one of the eight integral parts of the virtue of prudence is our memory.[8] How can we better use our memory of the past to make prudent decisions in the present moment?

---

8. Gregory Pine, *Prudence: Choose Confidently, Live Boldly* (Huntington, IN: Our Sunday Visitor, 2022), 77.

☐ 4. As we hear about discipline in both Sirach and Proverbs, how do we view discipline? Does the root of the word "discipline," to make a disciple of, change our view of how we discipline ourselves or those under our authority, such as our children?

☐ 5. In 1 Maccabees 13, we hear that the Jewish people achieve freedom. As they battle the Greeks they are sure to fight in a way that respects the Law of the Lord and their covenant with him. When we come in conflict with others, do we prioritize showing respect and follow the Law of the Lord in our disagreements?

Weekly Challenge
This week, visit the grave of a deceased loved one. Say a prayer at the grave site, and if possible, and if you feel called to, clean the site and bring flowers. If you do not live near the gravesites of any relatives or friends, visit a nearby cemetery and say a prayer for the souls of those buried there.

Group Activity
As we listen to the wisdom of Sirach, Fr. Mike reminds us that we become the average of the five people we spend the most time with. Sirach tells us to spend time with the virtuous so we may grow through their example. As a group, brainstorm five historical figures who would be virtuous companions today. What makes them people Sirach would recommend? Then, discuss how we can become better friends who help those around us grow in virtue.

Note of Hope

It's tempting to seek attention in conversations, but we forget the beauty and power of silence. Mary treasured the mysteries of the Incarnation in silence. Saints like Joseph and Catherine Labouré are venerated for their silence. When tempted to gossip, speak ill of others, or draw attention to ourselves, let us ask their intercession— those who treasured silence and reflected the beauty of the Silent One in his Passion.

SCRIPTURE VERSE TO REMEMBER

"Have you heard a word? Let it die with you.
Be brave! It will not make you burst!"
SIRACH 19:10

Prayer Intentions

Response (R): Lord, have mercy on me, a sinner.
When I am reluctant to forgive others: **R.**
In reparation for the times that I have gossiped: **R.**
When I desire not to get caught in my sin more than I desire not to sin at all: **R.**
When I choose selfishness over prudence: **R.**
When I disrespect others with whom I disagree: **R.**
In this year spent with your Word: **R.**

St. Callistus I,
pope and martyr, pray for us.
Feast Day: October 14

Catechism Connection

These paragraphs in the *Catechism* may be helpful for reflection on the Scripture read this week in *The Bible in a Year*: CCC 1040, 2214, 2468, 2544

Highlight from the *Catechism*:

- "The Last Judgment will reveal that God's justice triumphs over all the injustices committed by his creatures and that God's love is stronger than death" (CCC 1040).

Closing Prayer

Father in heaven, we give you praise and thanks for this day and your guiding Word. Guard our minds and thoughts, that all we say and do may be true, good, helpful, and wise. May everything we do bring you glory and bless those around us. In Jesus' name, we pray. Amen.

Opening Prayer

Father in heaven, thank you for a new day where you reveal your Word to us and help us to put it into practice. In Jesus' name, we pray. Amen.

Reflection with Scripture

☐ 1. In 1 Maccabees 14:12, we hear that Israel is able to rest from its enemies, even though there will be more fighting in the future. The same is true of our own lives. When we experience peaceful moments, we know that we are not exempt from future suffering. Do we choose to enter fully into the present moment's peace without worrying about the future? What actions can we take to acknowledge the blessings of the present moment?

☐ 2. The virtue of temperance means using the right thing, at the right time, in the right way. In what areas of my life, with what things, do I need to grow in temperance?

☐ 3. In Proverbs, we are warned against the spiritual effects of too much alcohol. How do these verses apply to the addictions we are tempted to? Often, addictions try to fill a void or wound in our hearts. What practical steps can we take to open our hearts to healing?

☐ 4. Sirach 40 makes the distinction between what is good and what is better. In this world that contains many good things, how can we choose the best things for our mind, heart, body, emotions, and soul?

☐ 5. Proverbs 24:16 reminds us that even the "righteous man falls seven times," yet he "rises again." How does this verse help protect us from discouragement?

Weekly Challenge

Sirach 37:13 says, "Establish the counsel of your own heart." Take time to meditate on Jesus' most Sacred Heart, the source of counsel to our own hearts. Pray this prayer to the Sacred Heart:

I give myself and consecrate to the Sacred Heart of our Lord Jesus Christ, my person and my life, my actions, pains, and sufferings, so that I may be unwilling to make use of any part of my being other than to honor, love, and glorify the Sacred Heart. ...

Be then, O Heart of goodness, my justification before God the Father, and turn away from me the strokes of his righteous anger. O Heart of love, I put all my confidence in you, for I fear everything from my own wickedness and frailty, but I hope for all things from your goodness and bounty.

Remove from me all that can displease you or resist your holy will; let your pure love imprint your image so deeply upon my heart, that I shall never be able to forget you or to be separated from you.

May I obtain from all your loving kindness the grace of having my name written in your Heart, for in you I desire to place all my happiness and glory, living and dying in bondage to you. Amen.

Group Activity

Sirach 37:13 tells us to "establish the counsel of your own heart." Discuss with the group how you would answer the questions. Fr. Mike encourages us to ponder this verse:

- Do I know my own heart?
- How do I hear the Lord's voice?
- What are the wounds of my heart?
- What are the inclinations of my heart?
- What are the holes, the gaps, the cracks in my heart?
- Where is my heart foolish?
- Where is my heart wise?

Note of Hope

The *Catechism* defines intercession as "a prayer of petition which leads us to pray as Jesus did." It continues, "Since Abraham, intercession—asking on behalf of another—has been characteristic of a heart attuned to God's mercy. The intercession of Christians recognizes no boundaries" (see CCC 2634–2636). When we intercede for others, we are imitating Jesus, attuning our hearts to his Heart. May we pray for those most in need of his mercy each day.

SCRIPTURE VERSE TO REMEMBER

"May he give you all a heart to worship him and to do his will with a strong heart and a willing spirit."

2 MACCABEES 1:3

Prayer Intentions

Response (R): O Lord, have mercy on your people.

As we seek to grow in the virtue of temperance: **R.**

When fear of death overcomes us: **R.**

That we may remember that your presence is always with us: **R.**

When we turn to your Sacred Heart: **R.**

When we have not obeyed your commands: **R.**

In this year spent with your Word: **R.**

St. Luke, pray for us, especially physicians, artists, and students.
Feast Day: October 18

Catechism Connection

These paragraphs in the *Catechism* may be helpful for reflection on the Scripture read this week in *The Bible in a Year*: CCC 1181, 1806, 2427, 2616

Highlight from the *Catechism*:

- "*Prudence* is 'right reason in action,' writes St. Thomas Aquinas, following Aristotle. It is not to be confused with timidity or fear, nor with duplicity or dissimulation … it guides the other virtues by setting rule and measure. It is prudence that immediately guides the judgment of conscience. The prudent man determines and directs his conduct in accordance with this judgment" (CCC 1806).

Closing Prayer

Father in heaven, we praise you and thank you for your Word and your presence in every moment. You hold us in being and in your arms. Help us never to slip from your grasp but to be firmly in your will and heart. In Jesus' name, we pray. Amen.

Opening Prayer

Father in heaven, we praise you and thank you for your Word, your grace, and your presence today. As we walk through the story of Israel's struggles, help us know when to fight, when to flee, and how to be faithful in every call. You are faithful and true—help us to be the same. In Jesus' name, we pray. Amen.

Reflection with Scripture

☐ 1. In 2 Maccabees 5, we read that the Israelites realize the trials they are undergoing are a sign that the Lord is teaching them and bringing them back to him. Do we see our trials as an opportunity for growing closer to God?

☐ 2. We hear of the heroic Jewish martyrs who are killed for following God's covenant and commands. The word *martyr* comes from a Greek word that means "witness." In what ways can we publicly witness our belief in God? How can we become greater witnesses of our Faith?

☐ 3. In 2 Maccabees 6, we hear the story about Eleazar, who refuses to give scandal to others by pretending to eat pork. This refusal costs him his life. Do I lead others into sin through my actions? Do I realize that my actions may have an impact on what others may do?

☐ 4. In 2 Maccabees 7, we hear about a mother who, after watching the torture and martyrdom of all of her seven sons, is martyred, too. Throughout the ordeal, the family members encourage one another to stay strong in their faith until the end. How can we imitate this beautiful family? How can we encourage the ones we love not to give up their faith, especially during times of pain and suffering?

☐ 5. The people of Israel realize that their courage comes from the Lord. Do we believe that God is the source of our true courage? How is our trust in God related to the gift of courage?

Weekly Challenge

This week, read about a saint who was martyred (such as St. Sebastian, St. Lucy, St. Teresa Benedicta of the Cross, or St. Maximilian Kolbe). What were his or her passions and interests? What impacts you the most about his or her story? In prayer, reflect on how you can live out a "white martyrdom" each day by witnessing to your faith without the shedding of your blood. Ask the saint whose life you read about to intercede for you.

Group Activity

Ahead of time, make a list of several martyrs with brief biographies, including their historical time and interesting facts. Share these stories with the group without revealing their names. Discuss what the stories have in common and what stands out. Reflect on how their stories inspire faithfulness to our Lord in our own circumstances. Invite group members to guess the saints' names. Did hearing the stories without names help connect their stories to our lives?

Note of Hope

Our lives are a gift meant to be poured out. Our world tells us we deserve comfort and that we should demand it and even expect it immediately. Yet instead of looking toward the world's comfort, we must instead look to our King on his throne, the Cross, a King who completely poured out his being for others—for us. He held nothing back. Our lives are about setting hearts ablaze for love of God.

SCRIPTURE VERSE TO REMEMBER

*"For even if for the present I should avoid
the punishment of men, yet whether I live or
die I shall not escape the hands of the Almighty."*
2 MACCABEES 6:26

Prayer Intentions

Response (R): Teach us to live according to your wisdom.
So that we may always see our trials as an opportunity to draw closer to you: **R.**
That we may always witness to you through our words and actions: **R.**
That we may always encourage others to live out their faith: **R.**
May we remember that you are the source of our courage: **R.**
In this year spent with your Word: **R.**

St. Anthony Mary Claret,
devoted to the Immaculate
Heart of Mary, pray for us.
Feast Day: October 24

Catechism Connection

These paragraphs in the *Catechism* may be helpful for reflection on the Scripture read this week in *The Bible in a Year*: CCC 992, 1505, 2518

Highlight from the *Catechism*:

- "The sixth beatitude proclaims, 'Blessed are the pure in heart, for they shall see God.' 'Pure in heart' refers to those who have attuned their intellects and wills to the demands of God's holiness, chiefly in three areas: charity; chastity or sexual rectitude; love of truth and orthodoxy of faith" (CCC 2518).

Closing Prayer

Father in heaven, we praise you and thank you. Hear the cries of our hearts—our pain, suffering, and longing. Let every desperate voice know you hear and care. Be with us now. Thank you for your Word and the Holy Spirit who fills, guides, and gives us courage. Help us take another step today. In Jesus' name, we pray. Amen.

Opening Prayer

Father in heaven, we praise and thank you for this day. Though we are fickle, you remain faithful—the rock and cornerstone. Lord Jesus, help us in our weakness and unsteadiness. Help us to see you each day and live by your power. In Jesus' name, we pray. Amen.

Reflection with Scripture

☐ 1. In chapter 13 of the book of Wisdom, we hear the foolishness of idolatry. Often, we are tempted to create idols out of created things. Fr. Mike challenges us to ask ourselves, "What or who is God's chief rival for my heart?" What steps can we take so that God has no rivals in our hearts?

☐ 2. As we begin the Gospel of Luke, we are reminded that many in our world see the Church as a bearer of "bad news"—about constraints, guilt, and a list of what they "cannot do." How can we better become bearers of the "Good News" of God's love and mercy for his people in a way that does not shy away from the truth, but rather "speaks truth in love"? (See Ephesians 4:15.)

☐ 3. In what ways do the response of Mother Mary and the response of Zechariah to the angel of the Lord differ?

☐ 4. Is there something in our lives that feels impossible? How can we take to heart the words of the angel Gabriel that God can do everything? (See Luke 1:37.)

☐ 5. Who is a person in my life right now that I need to go in "haste" to help? (See Luke 1:39.) How can I imitate Our Lady in bringing God's love to this person?

Weekly Challenge

In Luke 6, Jesus instructs us to love our enemies. Fr. Mike explains mercy as "love when we need to be loved the most, and we deserve to be loved the least." While mercy is often seen positively, Fr. Mike reminds us that in the ancient world, mercy was viewed as weakness. This week, ponder whether you see mercy as a virtue or a weakness. How would your life change if you grew in mercy?

Group Activity

Together as a group, look up Mary's Magnificat in the Bible in Luke 1:46–55. Pray it out loud. Afterward, discuss what verse stands out to you the most, and why.

Note of Hope

Mercy is an acknowledgment of the brokenness of man. It breaks through human sinfulness with the light of hope—the hope of salvation and betterment, the hope of sanctity and heaven. Deep love leads to deep mercy. God's love for us is a Merciful Love, which is transformative, renewing, and sanctifying. One of the greatest mysteries of his merciful love is that we can participate in it through accepting his love and mercy and, in turn, extending it to others.

SCRIPTURE VERSE TO REMEMBER

"And blessed is she who believed that there would be a fulfilment of what was spoken to her from the Lord."
LUKE 1:45

Prayer Intentions

Response (R): *Lord, in your great mercy, hear and answer us.*
In all the situations that we have called impossible, let us remember that nothing is impossible with you: *R.*
That we may grow in your Merciful Love: *R.*
That we may always echo the "yes" of Mother Mary: *R.*
That we may be bearers of your Good News each day: *R.*
That we may go gladly to serve all those in need: *R.*
For all of our intentions this year spent with your Word: *R.*

St. Charles Borromeo,
pray for us all,
especially for bishops.
Feast Day: November 4

Catechism Connection

These paragraphs in the *Catechism* may be helpful for reflection on the Scripture read this week in *The Bible in a Year*: CCC 722, 1847, 2833

Highlight from the *Catechism*:

- "God created us without us: but he did not will to save us without us. To receive his mercy, we must admit our faults" (CCC 1847).

Closing Prayer

Father in heaven, we praise and thank you for this day and your Word. We see your heart in Jesus, who loves the forgotten and even our enemies. Though we have rebelled, you loved us and gave your life for us. Help us to love as you love and live for you today and always. In Jesus' name, we pray. Amen.

Opening Prayer

Father in heaven, we praise and thank you. You are great, good, and faithful. Every day you give us new mercy. Help us receive your mercy and walk in it. Fill our hearts with your grace and love, so we become vessels of your love and conduits of your grace. We ask this in Jesus' name. Amen.

Reflection with Scripture

☐ 1. The lawyer wishing to justify himself asks Jesus, "Who is my neighbor?" (Luke 10:29). Jesus responds with the parable of the Good Samaritan and then asks the lawyer who in the story acted as a neighbor to the man who fell among the robbers (see Luke 10:29–37). How can we shift our perspective from expecting to be treated well by our neighbors to being a good neighbor ourselves?

☐ 2. Jesus tells us, "When your eye is sound, your whole body is full of light; but when it is not sound, your body is full of darkness" (Luke 11:34). Do the things we look at (books, magazines, videos, websites, concerts) reflect the light of Christ?

☐ 3. Do I rejoice in the conversion of others? Or do I, like the prodigal son's brother, grow angry when mercy that leads to conversion is shown?

☐ 4. From the Cross, Jesus forgives. How can we be more open to forgiveness in our own hearts?

☐ 5. During the walk to Emmaus after the Resurrection, Jesus tells the men that they have been "slow of heart to believe" (Luke 24:25). Do we show resistance to the Gospel message? How can we grow in eagerness to hear the Good News?

Weekly Challenge

Each day this week, slowly pray and ponder the words of the prayer Jesus taught his disciples, the Our Father:

Our Father who art in heaven, hallowed be thy name. Thy kingdom come. Thy will be done on earth, as it is in heaven. Give us this day our daily bread, and forgive us our trespasses, as we forgive those who trespass against us, and lead us not into temptation, but deliver us from evil. Amen.

At the end of the week, reflect on how this daily prayer impacted you.

Group Activity

This week, pray the Stations of the Cross together as a group. If you meet at a parish and have access to the church, you can pray before the Stations of the Cross in your church. If you meet outside a parish setting or if walking is difficult for any of your group members, you can pray along with Fr. Mark-Mary and Br. Juanmaría's video "Pray with Us: The Stations of the Cross," available for free on the Ascension Presents YouTube channel.

Note of Hope

Just as the father in the parable of mercy waited for his son, God waits to run toward you, embrace you, and offer his divine kiss of mercy (see Luke 15:20). The Father's merciful love anticipates our repentance. Every time we return to him, the feast of the prodigal son is renewed. When we choose to return, our sin becomes an occasion to experience his merciful love. "From misery to misery we go from mercy to mercy."[9]

SCRIPTURE VERSE TO REMEMBER

"Consider the lilies, how they grow; they neither toil nor spin;
yet I tell you, even Solomon in all his glory
was not clothed like one of these."
LUKE 12:27

Prayer Intentions

Response (R): With God, nothing will be impossible.

Help us live out our three-fold mission to deny ourselves, take up our cross daily, and follow you: *R.*

Help us remember the one thing that is needful when we are anxious in our work: *R.*

Help us to be a good neighbor to all: *R.*

Help us always return to you in gratitude, thanksgiving, and praise: *R.*

Help us when it is difficult to forgive: *R.*

In this year spent with your Word, let us hold on to the truth: *R.*

---

9. Pine, 65.

Catechism Connection

These paragraphs in the *Catechism* may be helpful for reflection on the Scripture read this week in *The Bible in a Year*: CCC 555, 638, 767, 786, 1692

Highlight from the *Catechism*:

- "Christ, King and Lord of the universe, made himself the servant of all, for he 'came not to be served but to serve, and to give his life as a ransom for many'" (CCC 786).

Closing Prayer

Father in heaven, we thank and praise you. Thank you for the Age of the Church and the gift of your Son and salvation. Thank you for the Holy Spirit dwelling in us, enabling prayer and transformation. Like the apostles united with Mary, we ask you to fill us with your Spirit today, that we may bring your Gospel and your presence to the world. In Jesus' name, we pray. Amen.

Opening Prayer

Father in heaven, we praise and thank you for your Word, your grace in Jesus Christ, and the Holy Spirit sent on Pentecost. Your Spirit works miracles and brings grace to us today. Help us receive your Spirit this day, keep us alive in your will, close to your heart, and never wandering from you. In Jesus' name, we pray. Amen.

Reflection with Scripture

☐ 1. In Acts 2:42, we hear that the newly baptized "held steadfastly to the apostles' teaching and fellowship, to the breaking of the bread and to the prayers." Do we hold steadfast to these four things, too? How can we grow in valuing each of these aspects of the Church and its mission?

☐ 2. Fr. Mike shares that the key word in Acts 4 is "boldness." Whether we consider ourselves bold or shy, how can we imitate the early Church's boldness in following Our Lord?

☐ 3. Reflecting on Romans 5:3, do we see our sufferings as fruitful? What steps can we take to choose to hope in God's love when we are suffering?

☐ 4. Romans 8:28 and Romans 8:38–39 promise us that nothing can separate us from the love of God. How can this reality change how we live and think about our circumstances? Do we allow ourselves to believe that God loves us so deeply?

☐ 5. St. Paul directs us to "not be conformed to this world" (Romans 12:2). How does the world's perspective hinder us from discerning God's will for us? How can we cooperate with God to "transform" and "renew" our understanding?

....

Weekly Challenge

Every day this week, pray for the gift of boldness. Ask God to increase this gift in you as he did for the apostles and early Church. Reflect on the areas in your life where you need to put this gift into action. Is there a situation or conversation that would benefit from your bold action or words? Ask the Holy Spirit to be with you as you discern what to do.

Group Activity

Together as a group, ask the Holy Spirit to be with you as you share your intentions and pray this prayer to him:

Oh Holy Spirit, you are the Third Person of the Blessed Trinity. You are the Spirit of truth, love, and holiness, proceeding from the Father and the Son, and equal to Them in all things. I adore you and love you with all my heart. Teach me to know and to seek God, by whom and for whom I was created. Fill my heart with a holy fear and a great love for him. Give me compunction and patience, and do not let me fall into sin.

Increase faith, hope, and charity in me and bring forth in me all the virtues proper to my state of life. Help me to grow in the four cardinal virtues, your seven gifts, and your twelve fruits. Amen.

Note of Hope

The Holy Spirit is our advocate, comforter, and guide. Our conversations, work, duties, and vocation would change in the most incredible ways if we made it a habit to call on his assistance each day in all we do. We would be set ablaze in his love, and so we would set hearts ablaze for love of him. May we, with the same boldness of the apostles, cry out, "Come, Holy Spirit!"

SCRIPTURE VERSE TO REMEMBER

"We know that in everything God works for good with those who love him, who are called according to his purpose."
ROMANS 8:28

Prayer Intentions

Response (R): Come, Holy Spirit, and renew the face of the earth!
That we may grow in boldness of spirit so as to proclaim you more:
R.
That we may cultivate fellowship in our communities and parish:
R.
So we remember that in everything God works for good with those who love him: **R.**
For the Church to grow in the gifts and fruits of the Spirit: **R.**
For all newly baptized Christians: **R.**
For all those preparing to receive the Sacraments: **R.**
In this year spent with your Word: **R.**

St. Rose Philippine Duchesne,
pray for missionaries
and for all of us.
Feast Day: November 18

Catechism Connection

These paragraphs in the *Catechism* may be helpful for reflection on the Scripture read this week in *The Bible in a Year*: CCC 731, 1996, 2011, 2473

Highlight from the *Catechism*:

- "*The charity of Christ is the source in us of all our merits before God. Grace, by uniting us to Christ in active love, ensures the supernatural quality of our acts and consequently their merit before God and before men*" (CCC 2011).

Closing Prayer

Father in heaven, we thank you and give you praise. Thank you for being with us today. Thank you for feeding us with your Word, with your Spirit. Thank you for being present to us and shaping our hearts and lighting them on fire. Help us to love you and to love our neighbor as ourselves. Help us to love each other well. In Jesus' name, we pray. Amen.

Reflection with Scripture

☐ 1. Saul, who has been persecuting the Church, hears Jesus say, "I am Jesus, whom you are persecuting" (Acts 9:5). Do we see the Church as Christ's body? Do we recognize that sinful actions that harm the Church are "persecuting" Christ himself? How can this truth affect our lives?

☐ 2. As Peter shares the Good News to the Gentiles, he says, "God shows no partiality" (Acts 10:34). In our relationships with others, even our friendships, do we show partiality? How can we love one another as Christ loves us?

☐ 3. The people in Lystra want to declare Paul and Barnabas gods when God heals a crippled man through Paul's intercession. Like Paul and Barnabas, how can we always direct our good works to God and glorify him, instead of trying to glorify ourselves and take the credit? How can we temper our pride and grow in humility when others want to glorify us instead of God?

☐ 4. In his first letter to the Corinthians, St. Paul reminds the people of Corinth that they are "called to be saints." When you interact with others, do you encourage them to become saints through the words you use and the way you act? Why is it important to encourage others in this way?

☐ 5. How can we glorify God in and through our bodies? Do we see our bodies as gifts? As good? As temples of the Holy Spirit? (See 1 Corinthians 5–6.)

Weekly Challenge

Each day this week, pray the "Come, Holy Spirit" prayer, invoking the intercession of the Holy Spirit, just as the members of the Early Church did. Each day, if possible, invite someone to pray this prayer with you.

Come, Holy Spirit,
fill the hearts of Thy faithful
and enkindle in them the fire of Thy love.
V. *Send forth Thy Spirit and they shall be created.*
R. *And Thou shalt renew the face of the earth.*
Let us pray. O God,
Who didst instruct the hearts of the faithful
by the light of the Holy Spirit,
grant us in the same Spirit to be truly wise,
and ever to rejoice in his consolation.
Through Christ our Lord. Amen.

Group Activity

Ask someone in the group to read 1 Corinthians 12 out loud. Discuss the gifts of the Holy Spirit. Invite each person to share one gift he or she especially appreciates and why. Finish by thanking God for these gifts and asking him to increase love in our hearts so that we may use our gifts for his glory.

Note of Hope

"To proclaim the Gospel and bear witness to the faith is more necessary than ever today," Pope Benedict XVI preached. "Presenting Christ is not imposing him. Twelve Apostles gave their lives to make Christ known and loved. The Gospel has spread through men and women inspired by that same missionary fervor. Today, there is a need for disciples who give their time and energy to serve the Gospel, responding generously to God's urgent call, as Blesseds and Saints have done."[10] May we, like the first apostles, have the boldness of heart to preach the Good News with urgency and joy of heart.

SCRIPTURE VERSE TO REMEMBER

"Do you not know that your body is a temple of the Holy Spirit within you, which you have from God? You are not your own."
1 CORINTHIANS 6:19

Prayer Intentions

Response (R): Glory be to you, Father, Son, and Spirit!
Open our hearts to receive all the spiritual gifts you have in store for us: *R.*
We pray for those members of the Church's body experiencing persecution: *R.*
Give us the strength to accompany our prayer with fasting: *R.*
Help us to glorify you always through the temple of our body: *R.*
We pray for our Church leaders: *R.*
Help us so that we may show no partiality in our love: *R.*
In this year spent with your Word, we pray: *R.*

10. Benedict XVI, Message to the Young People of the World on the Occasion of the 23rd World Youth Day (July 20, 2008), 7, vatican.va.

St. Cecilia, pray for musicians and for all of us.
Feast Day: November 22

Catechism Connection

These paragraphs in the *Catechism* may be helpful for reflection on the Scripture read this week in *The Bible in a Year*: CCC 1427, 791, 2003, 2632, 1818

Highlight from the *Catechism*:

- "The virtue of hope responds to the aspiration to happiness which God has placed in the heart of every man. It keeps man from discouragement; it sustains him during times of abandonment; it opens up his heart in expectation of eternal beatitude" (CCC 1818).

Closing Prayer

Father in heaven, we praise and thank you for your Word. Thank you for the challenges and questions it brings. In difficult moments, send your Holy Spirit through Jesus Christ to open our hearts and minds to your truth. Help us to trust you fully—in your Word and your will in our daily lives. We pray in Jesus' name. Amen.

Opening Prayer

Father in heaven, we praise and thank you for this day. Thank you for your constant presence, guidance, and help. We give you praise because you not only call us to love—you are love. Help us to love and trust you in every circumstance. We pray in Jesus' name. Amen.

Reflection with Scripture

☐ 1. As our culture is filled with a spirit of meaninglessness and pleasure-seeking that leads to unhappiness, what are practical ways to teach others that true joy comes from life in Christ, just as the apostles did?

☐ 2. Why is it important to resist the temptation to fit in with our culture? What are the repercussions if we try to fit in at the expense of our faith?

☐ 3. Many Christians do not invoke the power of the Holy Spirit; we live as though we have never encountered the Holy Spirit. What are practical, actionable ways that we can invite the Holy Spirit to be a part of our life, vocation, and work?

☐ 4. Is there something in my life that does not belong to a life lived in Christ? What is hindering me from entering God's kingdom and living his kingdom here and now? Am I willing to remove it? How can I uproot it? How would my life look different?

☐ 5. In 1 Corinthians 13, we hear how love is more excellent than all other gifts. After hearing the description of love, in what ways do we see that we can grow in this virtue?

Weekly Challenge

Calling to mind St. Paul's words in 2 Corinthians 9:7, "God loves a cheerful giver," ask the Holy Spirit to give you the gift of cheer and joy when you serve others this week. Take note of how your cheerfulness affects both you and others this week.

Group Activity

Together, inviting the Holy Spirit to be present in your prayer, pray the Act of Faith.

O my God, I firmly believe
that you are one God in three divine Persons,
Father, Son, and Holy Spirit.
I believe that your divine Son became man
and died for our sins and that he will come
to judge the living and the dead.
I believe these and all the truths
which the Holy Catholic Church teaches
because you have revealed them
who are eternal truth and wisdom,
who can neither deceive nor be deceived.
In this faith I intend to live and die. Amen.

Note of Hope

The great missionaries show that God's love is stronger than any force. Language barriers, illness, distance, and time cannot stop a heart united to Merciful Love from proclaiming Christ. Christ is proclaimed in our sacrificial love, merciful forgiveness, and smile. He is proclaimed when we wash floors, intercede for others, and unite our sufferings to him. In every action, we can choose to be missionaries for Christ, hoping for a heavenly crown and to see the fruit of our mission.

SCRIPTURE VERSE TO REMEMBER

"For this slight momentary affliction is preparing for us an eternal weight of glory beyond all comparison."
2 CORINTHIANS 4:17

Prayer Intentions

Response (R): Grant them abundant blessings, Lord.
For those who are seeking you and desire to enter into full communion with you: *R.*
For all cheerful givers: *R.*
For those who work in ministry: *R.*
For those who call upon the Holy Spirit in their vocations, duties, and work: *R.*
For those who excel in the virtue of love: *R.*
For all those close to us during this year spent with your Word: *R.*

St. Nicholas, pray for children, sailors, merchants, and for us all.

Feast Day: December 6

Catechism Connection

These paragraphs in the *Catechism* may be helpful for reflection on the Scripture read this week in *The Bible in a Year*: CCC 1227, 1473, 1511

Highlight from the *Catechism*:

- "The believer enters through Baptism into communion with Christ's death, is buried with him, and rises with him ... Through the Holy Spirit, Baptism is a bath that purifies, justifies, and sanctifies" (CCC 1227).

Closing Prayer

Father in heaven, we give you praise and glory. We thank you for this day and for your Word. So often we forget who you are and who we are in your name. Lord God, you are present and active in every circumstance and season of our lives. Please help us to give you permission to do what you are trying to accomplish in us this day, in Jesus' name. Amen.

WEEK 50: DAYS 344–350

Reflection with Scripture

☐ 1. In 2 Corinthians 12:7, we hear about the "thorn" of St. Paul—something painful that he repeatedly prayed to be freed from. Are we able to accept our weaknesses humbly? How can we lean into God's ever-available love, mercy, and grace instead of relying on our own strength?

☐ 2. "For freedom Christ has set us free" (Galatians 5:1). Do I see my sins as a form of slavery? Do I desire a life of freedom? Or do I continue to turn to sin out of a sense of comfort and familiarity? How can I continually strive to free myself from the yoke of sin?

☐ 3. St. Paul entreats the Galatians to "bear one another's burdens" (Galatians 6:2). How can we, as the Church, grow in bearing one another's burdens with joy? How can we better work toward anticipating the needs of others and outdoing one another in love?

☐ 4. How can we understand St. Paul's guidance for Christian husbands and wives in Ephesians 5:21–33 through the paradigm of Christ's humble and sacrificial love for his Bride, the Church?

☐ 5. St. Paul encourages the Philippians to "let your manner of life be worthy of the gospel of Christ" (Philippians 1:27). Do we live life in a manner that is "worthy of the gospel?" What areas of our lives do we need to align to the Gospel message?

Weekly Challenge

Read Galatians 5:16–25. In prayer, ask yourself if there is a work of the flesh that you struggle with. Make an action plan to combat that vice this week. Each day, review how well you have implemented your action plan and pray for an increase in the fruits of the Spirit.

Group Activity

With your group, read Ephesians 6:10–18 aloud. What spiritual "armor of God" do we wear? Discuss what a spiritual "combat" plan might look like—daily prayer, fasting, daily Mass, an annual house blessing, wearing a scapular or medal. Are outward signs helpful in spiritual battle? What spiritual practices can we implement? Invite each group member to write down one to three actionable steps from this discussion.

Note of Hope

Prayer animates our life and gives us grace to love and show mercy. Growth in virtue—faith, hope, and love—is the fruit of prayer. Jesus teaches us how to pray and unites us to him as we pray. Before his mission, miracles, and offering his Body and Blood, Jesus prayed. In his suffering on the Cross, he prayed. The great saints make Jesus' prayer their own. Let us never let a day go by without prayer.

SCRIPTURE VERSE TO REMEMBER

"Finally, brethren, whatever is true, whatever is honorable, whatever is just, whatever is pure, whatever is lovely, whatever is gracious, if there is any excellence, if there is anything worthy of praise, think about these things."
PHILIPPIANS 4:8

Prayer Intentions

Response (R): For me, to live is Christ!
May we run the race and fight the good fight of faith: *R.*
May we cast aside all the works of the flesh: *R.*
May we grow in the fruits of the Spirit: *R.*
May we always ponder whatever is true, honorable, just, pure, lovely, gracious, excellent, and worthy of praise: *R.*
May we be content in whatever state we are in: *R.*
In this year spent with your Word, may we forever proclaim: *R.*

Catechism Connection

These paragraphs in the *Catechism* may be helpful for reflection on the Scripture read this week in *The Bible in a Year*: CCC 164, 820, 852, 1815, 1742

Highlight from the *Catechism*:

- "The gift of faith remains in one who has not sinned against it. But 'faith apart from works is dead': when it is deprived of hope and love, faith does not fully unite the believer to Christ and does not make him a living member of his Body" (CCC 1815).

Closing Prayer

Father in heaven, we give you praise and glory. Thank you for another day and this next step. We ask you to help us put your instruction into action. Help us to be not only hearers but doers of your Word. Let this time spent listening not simply wash over us but transform us. Help us put the love in our hearts into action. In Jesus' name, we pray. Amen.

Reflection with Scripture

☐ 1. James 4:7–8 reminds us, "Resist the devil and he will flee from you. Draw near to God and he will draw near to you." What are spiritual practices that help us "resist the devil"? What are some practical ways we can "draw near to God"?

☐ 2. In 1 Peter 2:9 we hear that we are "God's own people." Do we identify ourselves as Christians? Is that our most important identity?

☐ 3. St. Paul encourages the Colossians to "continue steadfastly in prayer, being watchful in it with thanksgiving" (Colossians 4:2). How are prayer and thanksgiving connected? How would we benefit if we joined our prayer with thanksgiving?

☐ 4. The three theological virtues, faith, love, and hope, "dispose Christians to live in a relationship with the Holy Trinity" (CCC 1812). What are some ways we can practice these three virtues each day within our own vocations?

☐ 5. The first letter of John reminds us that we cannot belong both to the world and to God (see 1 John 2:15). How can we use the gifts of the world and creation in a way that glorifies God?

....

Weekly Challenge
This week, set aside some time each day to read the *Catechism* or another book that will help you "be prepared to make a defense to any one who calls you to account for the hope that is in you" (1 Peter 3:15).

Group Activity
Discuss the reasons for our hope as Christians.
Begin by praying the Apostles' Creed, expressing our Faith together out loud:

I believe in God, the Father almighty, Creator of heaven and earth, and in Jesus Christ, his only Son, our Lord, who was conceived by the Holy Spirit, born of the Virgin Mary, suffered under Pontius Pilate, was crucified, died and was buried; he descended to hell; on the third day he rose again from the dead; he ascended into heaven, and is seated at the right hand of God the Father almighty; from there he will come to judge the living and the dead. I believe in the Holy Spirit, the holy catholic Church, the communion of saints, the forgiveness of sins, the resurrection of the body, and life everlasting. Amen.

Then, invite group members to share what they would say if someone asked them to account for their beliefs and hopes. Offer encouragement and help to anyone who is not sure how to express his or her hope.

Note of Hope

We are completely absolved of all our sins when we run to Christ and his Merciful Love in the Sacrament of Reconciliation. We are called to be saints, to cast out our nets into the deep, exchanging sinfulness for abundant grace. Let us not allow fear, anxiety, or pride to stop us from confessing and receiving forgiveness. Turn to our Merciful Savior to begin life anew, conquer sin, and become a source of his love for the world.

SCRIPTURE VERSE TO REMEMBER

"Above all hold unfailing your love for one another, since love covers a multitude of sins."
1 PETER 4:8

Prayer Intentions

Response (R): Lord, help us love as you love!

That we may always resist the temptations of the Evil One through our love: *R.*

That we may rejoice in our sufferings, knowing that we are participating in the great love of your Passion: *R.*

That we may always be prepared to give a reason for our hope: *R.*

That we may serve those we are tempted to ignore: *R.*

That we may remove the beam in our own eye first: *R.*

That we may increase in the virtue of love as we spend this year with your Word: *R.*

Catechism **Connection**

St. John of the Cross, pray for us all, especially those in the Carmelite Order.
Feast Day: December 14

These paragraphs in the *Catechism* may be helpful for reflection on the Scripture read this week in *The Bible in a Year*: CCC 1611, 1825, 2013, 2015, 2479

Highlight from the *Catechism*:

- "The way of perfection passes by way of the Cross. There is no holiness without renunciation and spiritual battle. Spiritual progress entails the ascesis and mortification that gradually lead to living in the peace and joy of the Beatitudes: He who climbs never stops going from beginning to beginning, through beginnings that have no end. He never stops desiring what he already knows" (CCC 2015).

Closing Prayer

Father in heaven, we give you praise and glory. We thank you for your Word. Thank you for making us into your children in your beloved Son, Jesus Christ. We ask you to please help us to walk in faith, hope, and love in all things, in all ways. In Jesus' name, we pray. Amen.

Reflection with Scripture

☐ 1. The letter of Jude may seem harsh to us. How can we read this letter not as a message of condemnation, but rather as a message to impel us to grow?

☐ 2. In 2 Timothy 4:7, we hear St. Paul express to Timothy, "I have fought the good fight." How can we persevere like St. Paul so that at the end of our lives we may faithfully and boldly echo his words?

☐ 3. As we hear the description of faith in Hebrews 11:1, "Faith is the assurance of things hoped for, the conviction of things not seen," in what ways can you grow in the virtue of faith?

☐ 4. In Revelation 2:4–5, we are pointed back to "the love you had at first." What can we do to cultivate our love for God each day instead of growing lukewarm and drifting away from that love?

☐ 5. What is the biggest impact that listening to the Bible has made on our lives? What is one thing we plan to implement from this experience?

Weekly Challenge

Commit to one way that you can continue to incorporate the Word of God in your life each day. Some ideas include attending daily Mass, reading the daily Mass readings each morning, praying the Liturgy of the Hours, starting a Bible study with your friends or at your parish, or reading and praying with a Bible verse each day.

Group Activity

Pray a Rosary together as a group, in thanksgiving for completing *The Bible in a Year*. Ask for the grace to continue to live and grow in God's Word each day. Share what impacted you the most from this year and how hearing the Good News of the Bible has changed you. Remember to continue to pray for your group members and thank them for journeying through the Bible with you this year.

WEEK 52: DAYS 358-365

Note of Hope

Let Christ love you. If your heart has been injured or is being hurt now, run to the Sacred Heart. His Heart is safe. Christ always brings healing. When we firmly choose love in union with Jesus' Sacred Heart, our own heart is strengthened to such a degree that nothing can separate us from his love. His love becomes our love, his mercy becomes our mercy. Remember that he will never abandon you. He wants to spend eternal life with you. You are his. You are loved.

SCRIPTURE VERSE TO REMEMBER

"And he who sat upon the throne said, 'Behold, I make all things new.' Also he said, 'Write this, for these words are trustworthy and true.'"
REVELATION 21:5

Prayer Intentions

Response (R): Lord, you are the King of our hearts!
We pray for all those who have listened to *The Bible in a Year*, that your Word may reign in their lives: *R.*
We pray for those who will listen to *The Bible in a Year* in the future, that their hearts may be open to your Word: *R.*
We pray for those who have yet to encounter you and your Word: *R.*
We pray in thanksgiving for this year spent with your Word: *R.*

St. John the Apostle, pray for us all, especially theologians and authors.
Feast Day: December 27

Catechism Connection

These paragraphs in the *Catechism* may be helpful for reflection on the Scripture read this week in *The Bible in a Year*: CCC 67, 81, 83, 890

Highlight from the *Catechism*:

- "*Sacred Scripture* is the speech of God as it is put down in writing under the breath of the Holy Spirit" (CCC 81).

Closing Prayer

Father in heaven, thank you. In Jesus' name, receive our thanks. Amen.